ARTISTS TREADING WATER
Defining the Flint Water Crisis through Art

Gale Glover, Will Alston, Jjenna Hupp Andrews, Katrina Bolton, Alicia Carey, Anthony Carey (age 3), Jim Cheek, Leon Collins, Christina Cuba, Malaya Cuba (age 4), Traci Currie, Robert Downer, Pauly M. Everett, Davontae Glenn (age 9), Caleb Glover (age 7), Percy Glover, Amy Hartwig, Jacob Johnson, Rhonda Jones, Janice McCoy, Kamariya Miller (age 7), Carrie Riley, Ashley Thornton

Front cover image: Dr. Jjenna Hupp Andrews
Front cover designer: Gale Glover via cover creator

Glover Publishing and Community Outsourcing (GPCO)

GloverPCO@gmail.com

DEDICATION

Thank you to all the artists for their contributions and dedication to the Flint community in bringing awareness and aiding in the recovery of the Flint Water Crisis.

FLINT WATER CRISIS

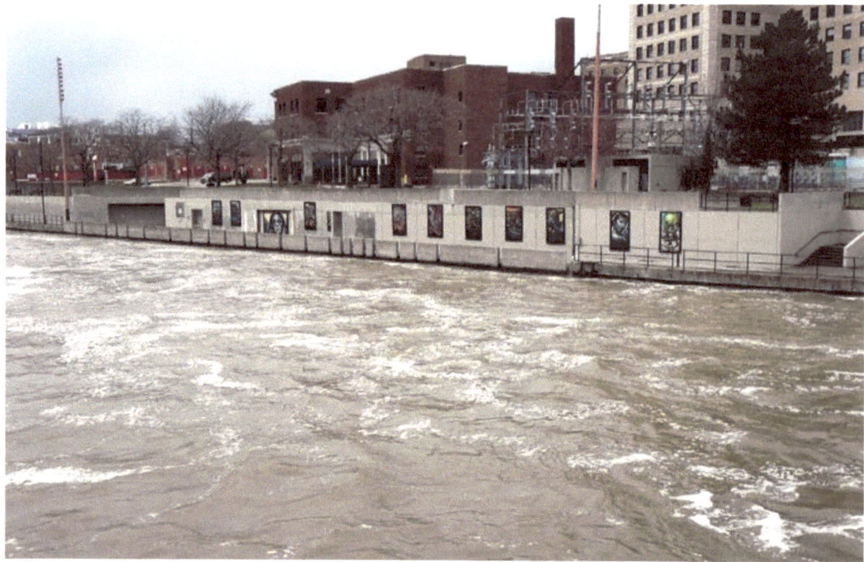

Photographer Jim Cheek

Beautifully illustrated art lines the wall adjacent to the Flint River. You cannot tell by looking at it but the river, its content, and its role in the recent massacre has been the topic of discussion for the past three years. The Flint Water system transfer systematically destroyed an infrastructure while contaminating more than 100,000 Flint residents including children. The lead-tainted water created disease, death, and destruction.

However, through its pain, the city has found peace in the form of artistic expression. Flint, Michigan is by far one of the strongest, most talented, and least recognized cities in the world. The talent that resides here is like no other and their ability to turn pain into a painting, death into passion, and destruction into beauty is why I am proud to call Flint my hometown. Photographers, painters, graphic designers, poets, spoken word artists, creative writers, authors and children banded together to share their story of a better future in spite of the destruction caused by their government. Artistic heroism to say the least.

–Author Gale Glover

"True freedom requires the rule of law and justice, and a judicial system in which the rights of some are not secured by the denial of rights to others."

--Jonathan Sacks

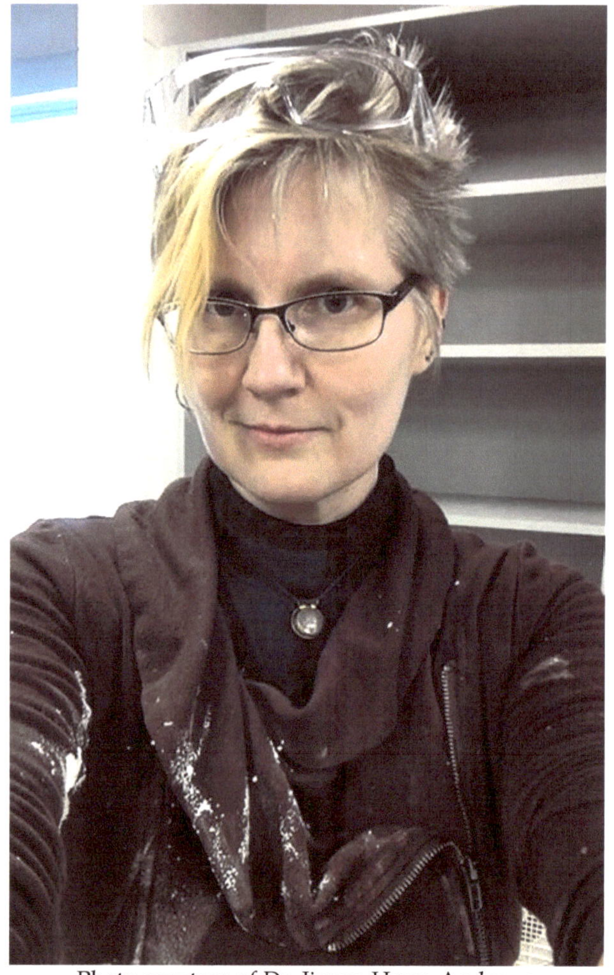
Photo courtesy of Dr. Jjenna Hupp Andrews

Dr. Jjenna Hupp Andrews, an innovative pioneer in recycling through art.

--Author Gale Glover

Dr. Jjenna Hupp Andrews is an Assistant Professor of Studio Art at Mott Community College in Flint Michigan, where she teaches Sculpture and Art Foundation courses. Dr. Andrews received her BFA in Metalsmithing/3D and MFA in Sculpture from Central Michigan University. She earned her Ph.D. in Interdisciplinary Studies, with a concentration Humanities and Society and a focus on visual/media culture and critical visual literacy at Union Institute & University. She was a Lecturer II in the Department of Fine Arts & Art History at The University of Michigan - Flint, for over 13 years, and adjunct faculty at Delta College for over 12 years, where she taught a variety of Studio Art, Art History, and Art Appreciation courses.

In addition to trying to keep up with her three daughters and husband, she is a mixed media and installation artist working mostly with a variety of fibers, metals, and found materials. Her current sculptural work uses the figural form to explore empathy and one's skin as a permeable membrane allowing for varying intensities of connection between the self and other. She has also working on two series of drawings: SAYHERNAME, which is a series of portraits of Transwomen of color who have been murdered in 2017, and “Suffer the Little Children…” which is a series of portraits of children in Syria, Iraq, and Yemen war zones and refugee camps.

Dr. Andrews' interdisciplinary visual and scholarly research interests focus on the social efficacy of visual and performance art as well as visual/media literacy in higher education, the intersections between the fine art and media realms, and how visual art and media can be used to engage with diversity/difference and most importantly, with issues of social justice. Her focus as a scholar-educator is always on how we can best facilitate student learning, critical thinking, and students' engagement with the world around them and how they can make a difference in this world.

She is currently at the beginning stages of a project that will take her and eventually some of her students, into area prisons to facilitate art and writing workshops with the incarcerated populations.

Dr. Jjenna Hupp Andrews

...and the children shall inherit the land flowing with milk and honey

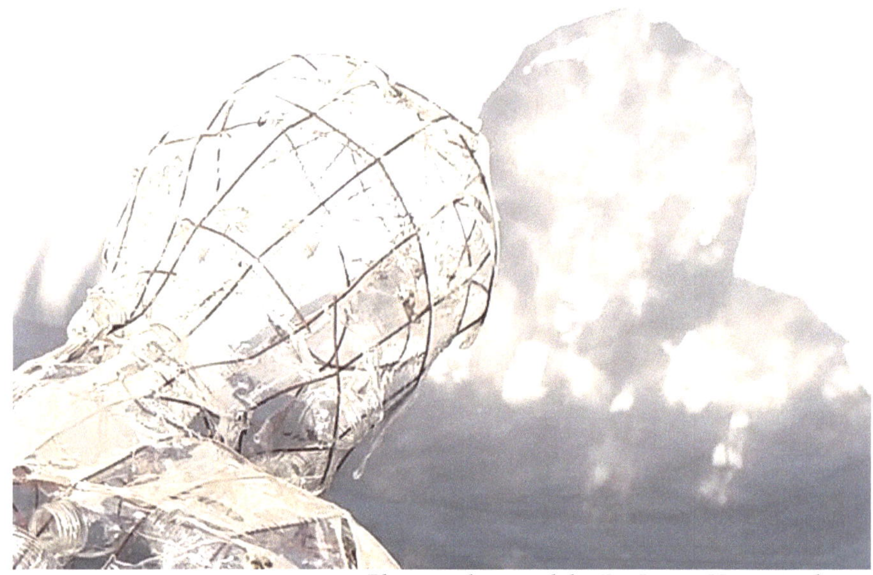

Photo and artwork by Dr. Jjenna Hupp Andrews

Water is our lifeblood: our bodies are made from it; our daily life depends on it; our spirits draw nourishment from it. In Michigan, we are surrounded by water; it defines who we are as a state and as a people. Yet, it seems, we are the first to take our water for granted. ...and the children shall inherit the land flowing with milk and honey... was an art installation at Buckham Gallery, which explored our water, the essence of life. Water is a spiritual as well as a physical medium that sustains and nurtures all the inhabitants (past, present, and future) of this fragile earth. It is life, always touching even when the cool, wet, life-blood is not felt upon our skin. Our ancestral memory and myth whisper to us the power and sacredness of water. It tells us we are born of water and we are carrying into the afterlife upon water. We are cleansed by immersion in water. Water is a vehicle of spiritual transformation.

These ripples of water sustaining our body spirit and soul are often unseen, unacknowledged or worse, ignored. We now bottle and sell our water with barely a second thought. In the last decade, Ice Mountain became the symbol of our culture's commodification of our life-blood. Industry extracts, contains, and exports spring and glacial water out of Michigan's (our earth's) aquifers (subsidized by the State). In the last year, water continuing to be understood by our government as a commodity, or, worse, purported to be a way to save money, has resulted in the poisoning of a city, our city. The once great city of Flint is in the midst of a painful rebirth; she is a phoenix struggling her way out of the fire to emerge stronger, more vital than ever. Her rebirth has been hindered; her life-sustaining yolk, tainted. Her most vulnerable populations made even more vulnerable, her people viewed as inconsequential. Water treated carelessly while ignoring legislated safeguards… all in the name of money.

We are connected; veins of water connect us. Now our life-blood carries the life-altering element of lead into our most sacred bodies, our children. The lead-heavy water intermingles with the blood until the two are forever inseparable, forever influencing, and at times hindering, the rhythms of our bodies. The children will carry this heaviness in their blood, causing challenges yet unknown, for the rest of their days. This moment's political implications of water are undeniable and inseparable from the social and spiritual. Michigan's water is being pumped and sold at the expense of the natural environment; Flint's water is contaminated, poisoning our brothers and sisters and children. Our life-blood is abused for short-term profit, and to the long-term detriment. Rivers and wells run dry, populations are poisoned, and politicians seek to protect their own as they quietly began to drink the clear, imported water from plastic bottles, the same bottles that deplete our clean aquafers.

Now our sacred life-blood must be carried into our poisoned city to healthfully sustain those the love of money has poisoned. Our life-blood is portioned out in cups, bowls, and bottles, leaving our future generations with only a memory of the water that once was… and our children shall inherit…

--Jjenna Hupp Andrews, Ph.D., M.F.A.

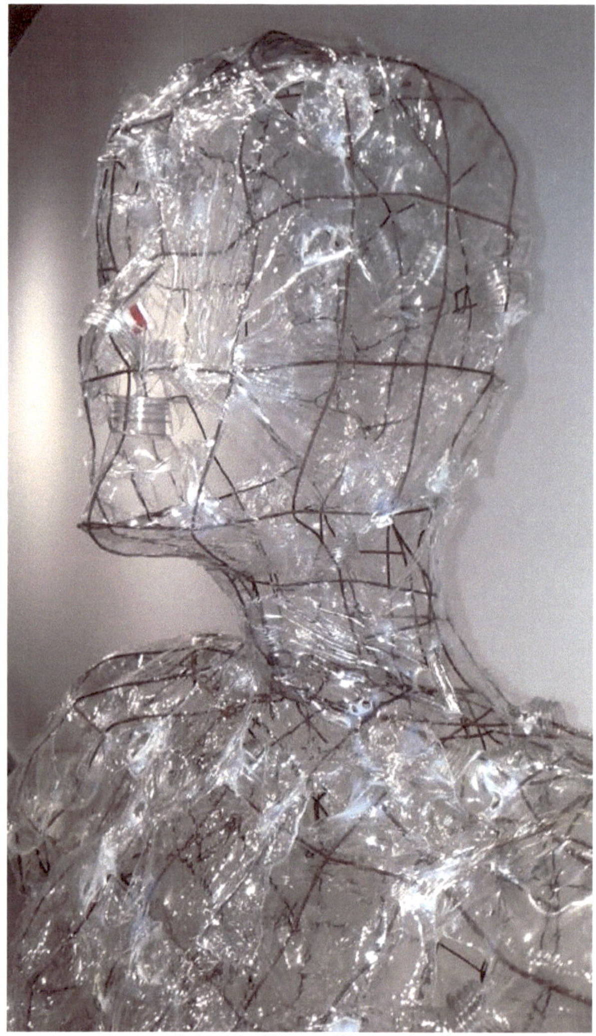
Artwork by Dr. Jjenna Hupp Andrews

Dr. Jjenna Hupp Andrews was instrumental in finding innovative and positive solutions to counter the excessive amounts of empty water bottles as a result of the Flint Water Crisis. She used recycling as a base to create artwork out of melted bottles and helped to provide answers as to what should be done with the used jugs when recycling storage space became a concern. **Dr. Jjenna Hupp Andrews, an innovative pioneer in recycling through art.**

--Author Gale Glover, Ed.S, MPA

OVERTURNED BY LEAD

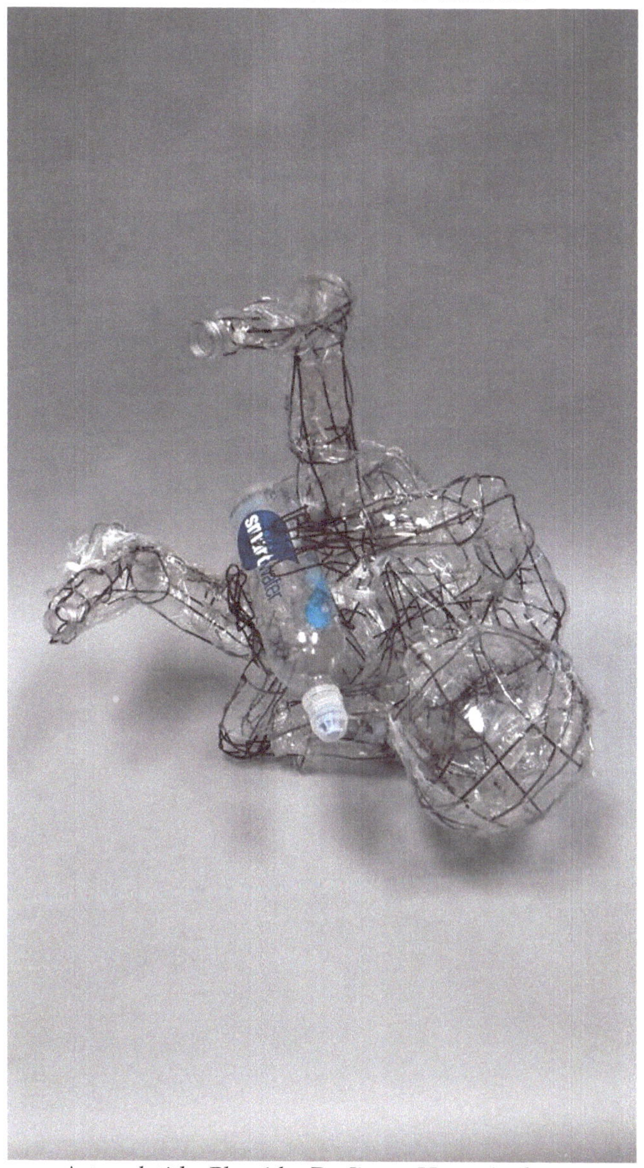

Artwork title: Play 1 by Dr. Jjenna Hupp Andrews

"**Injustice** anywhere is a threat to **justice** everywhere."

--Dr. Martin Luther King Jr.

DROWNING IN WATER BOTTLES

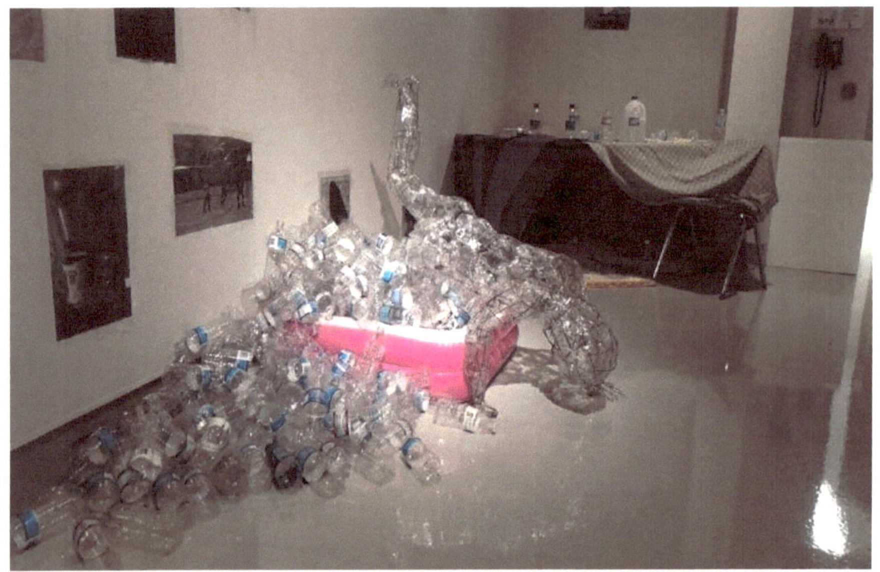

Artwork title: Bath by Dr. Jjenna Hupp Andrews

"Justice delayed is justice denied."
--William E. Gladstone

LIFE AND DEATH

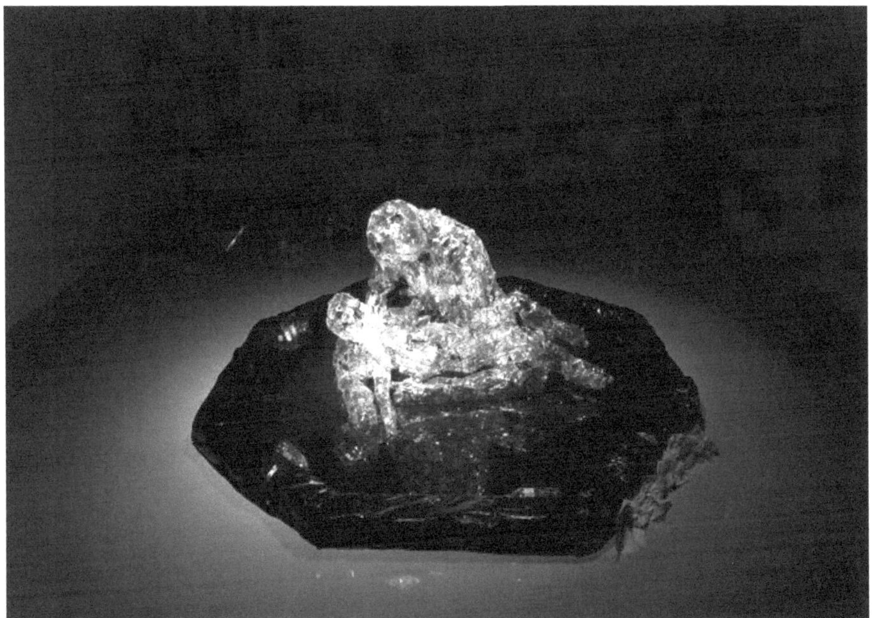

Artwork title: Flint Pieta 2 by Dr. Jjenna Hupp Andrews

In this picture, we see what looks to be a lifeless body. Maybe a child being held by a parent...possibly making the transition to the next stage in life...death. During the Flint Water Crisis, many lost their lives or experienced unrepairable damage. Physical and mental distress, financial hardships, and distrust of the government are just a few of the injustices that the Flint residents had to face. Dr. Jjenna Hupp Andrews life-size sculpture made from melted water bottles accurately tells the story of those in Flint who endured the water crisis.

However, the transition from life to death was not a natural occurrence for those who died as a result of the water crisis but a destruction created by the government. The Flint Water Crisis was said to be one of the biggest man-made disasters in U.S. History.

--Author Gale Glover

"Until the great mass of the **people** shall be filled with the sense of **responsibility** for each other's welfare, **social justice** can never be attained."

--Helen Keller

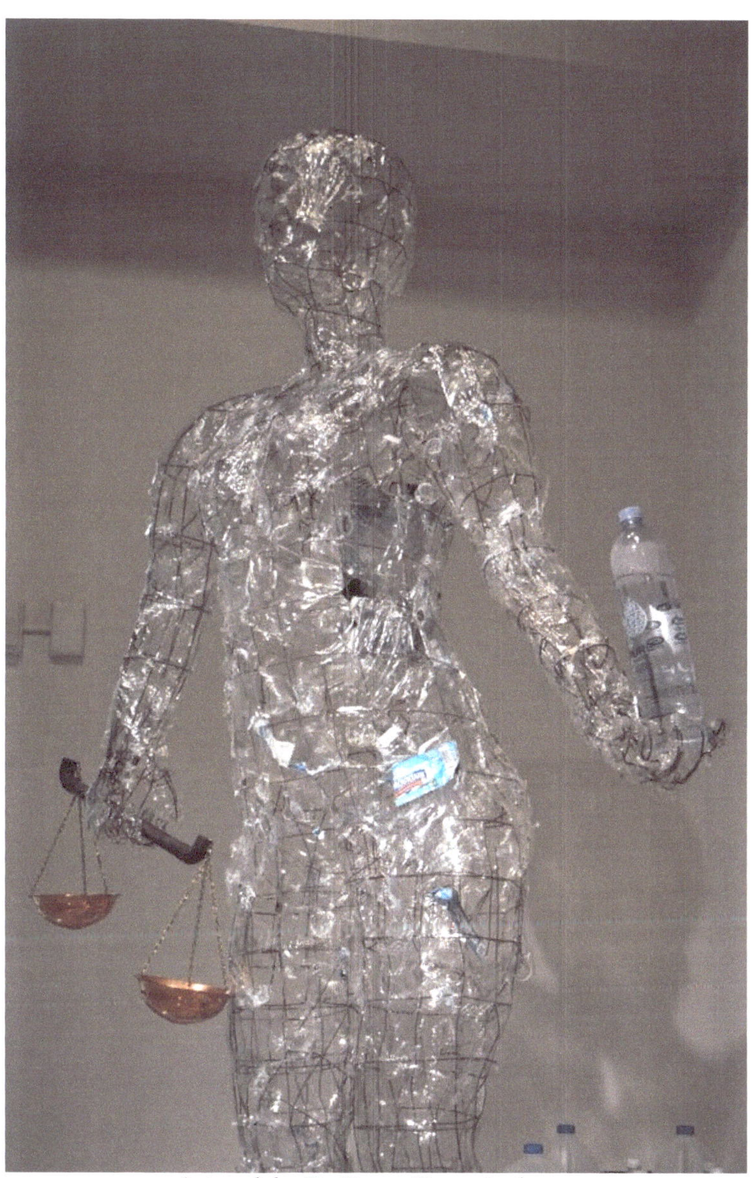

Artwork by Dr. Jjenna Hupp Andrews

"Where **justice** is denied, where poverty is enforced, where **ignorance** prevails, and where any one class is made to feel that society is an organized **conspiracy** to **oppress**, rob and degrade them, neither person nor property will be safe."

--Frederick Douglas

FLINT KIDS MATTER
7 YEAR OLD AUTHOR CALEB GLOVER

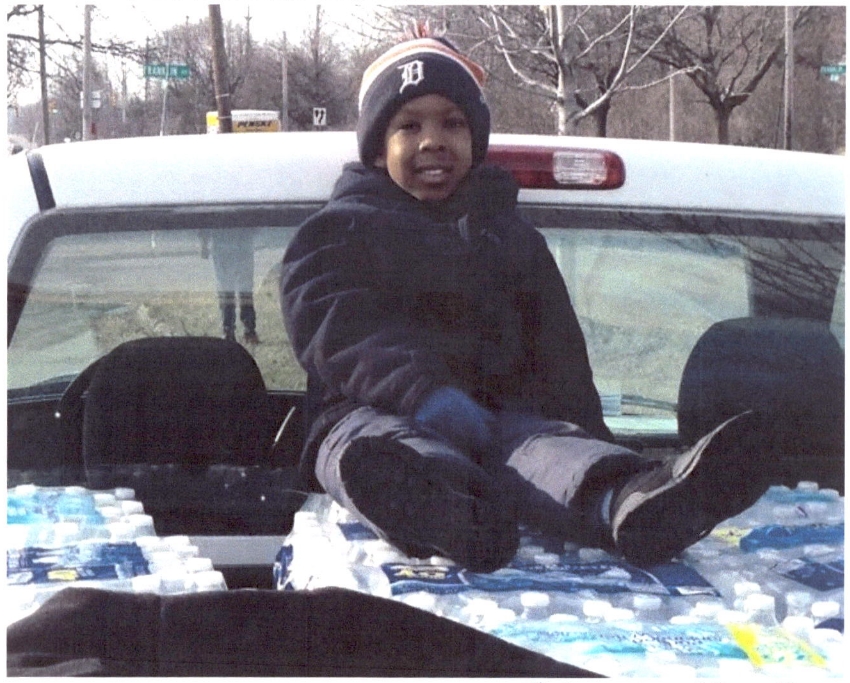

Photo courtesy of Percy Glover

The picture above shows a then 6-year-old Caleb Glover as he takes a break on a stack of water bottles on the back of his dad's truck. Caleb along with other Flint children volunteered at a water distribution site held at My Brother's Keeper, a nearby local Flint shelter. Caleb stated, "I remember that day. I was tired". When asked why he was passing out water Caleb replied, "To help people."

Spoken like a true hero, a now 7-year-old Caleb shared his thoughts about the water crisis.

--Author Gale Glover

A VOLUNTEER WE CAN BE PROUD OF!

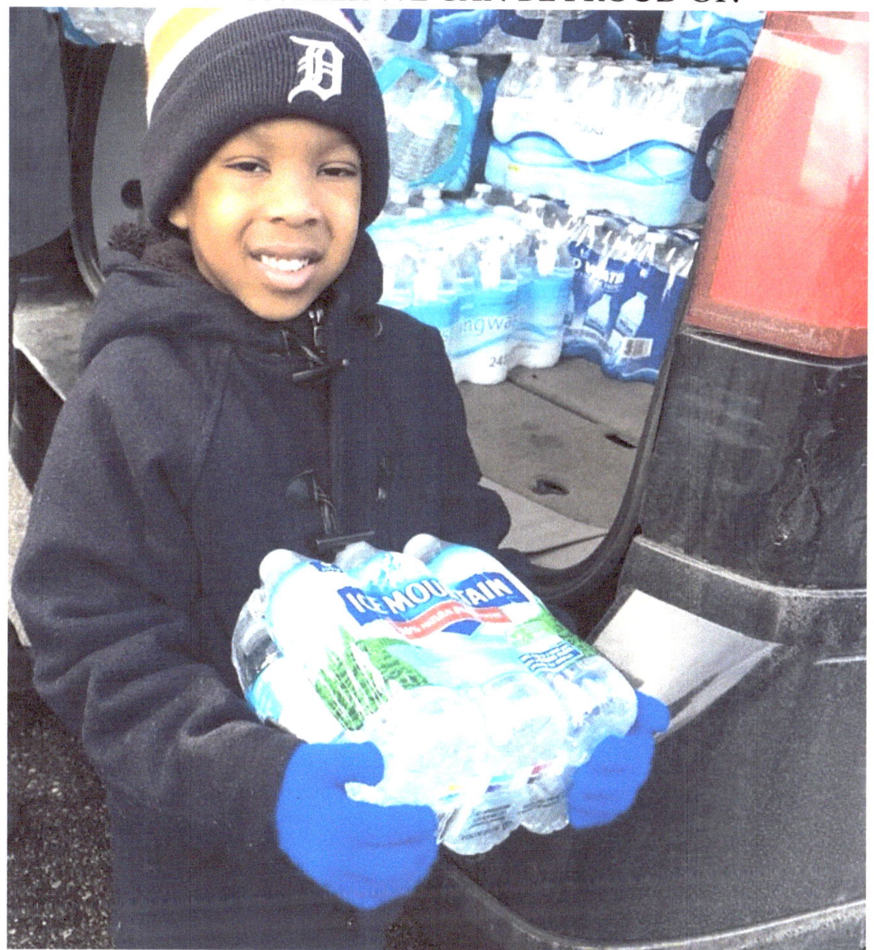

Photo courtesy of Percy Glover

"The water is bad, it is bad for your body and they should probably fix it."

--7 Year Old Author Caleb Glover

7 YEAR OLD AUTHOR KAMARIYA MILLER

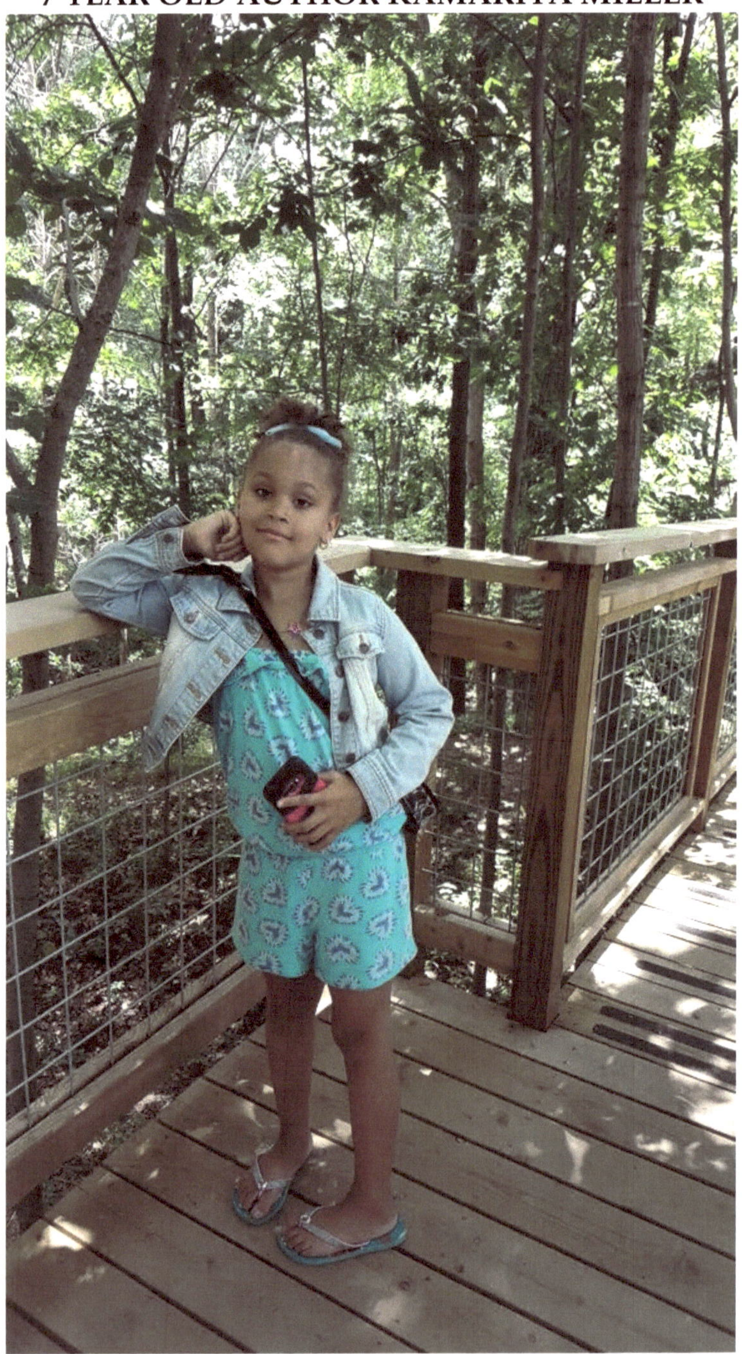

Photo courtesy of Katrina Bolton

WHY OH, WHY?
By Kamariya Miller

Why Oh why;
Did it have to happen to them?
What did they ever do to you? What could you do for them?
Why Oh why?
Must they live their lives this way?
With so much hurt and with so much pain.
Frankly Sir, You should be ashamed!
Why Oh, Why?
Did their lives must change?
Can they ever recover? Can they heal? Can you erase their pain?
Would they ever be happy, again? Can they ever play?
Why Oh, Why?

"The kids of Flint don't deserve to have bad water; they deserve to have good water; like everybody else"
– 7 Year old Author Kamariya Miller

9 YEAR OLD AUTHOR DAVONTAE GLENN

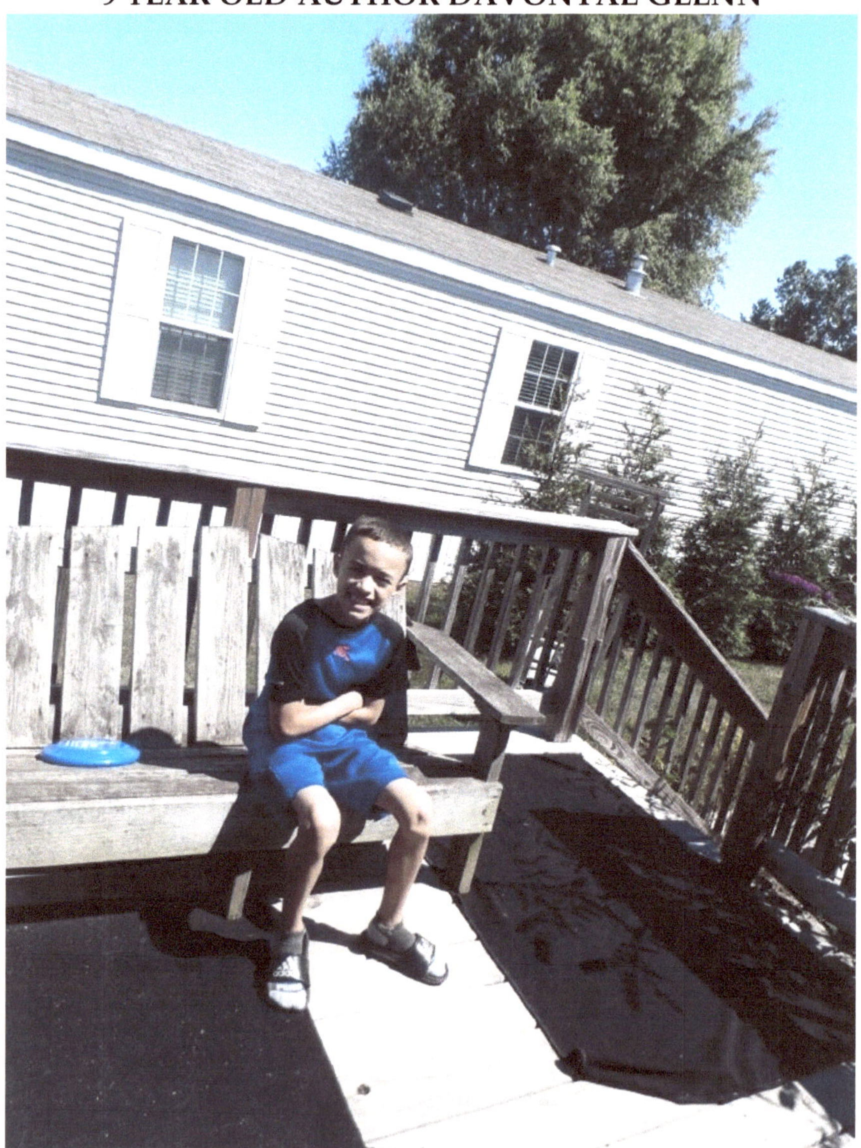

Photo courtesy of Katrina Bolton

9 year old Author Davontae Glenn wants to attend the University of Michigan-Flint and was excited to share his thoughts about the Flint Water Crisis and how it is affecting his hometown of Flint, Michigan.

--Author Gale Glover

How I feel about the Flint Water Crisis

When I think about the Flint Water Crisis, I get sad. Because the children in Flint cannot enjoy their time off from school and all the fun that summertime brings. They can't play in the water because their water has lead in it. They can't take a bath in clean water and they can't have outside water fights. They can't play with water balloons, go to local swimming pools or drink out of a water hose. All because the officials didn't do their job properly. It's not fair to the kids.

In school, we are taught that when we vote people into office that those people are supposed to protect us and help to make our lives better. What happened? Why, aren't their lives better? It's obvious that they made the children of Flint lives miserable and caused them to be unhappy. Which is a sad and bad thing to do.

--9 year old Author Davontae Glenn

HONESTY AND INNOCENCE
4 YEAR OLD AUTHOR MALAYA CUBA

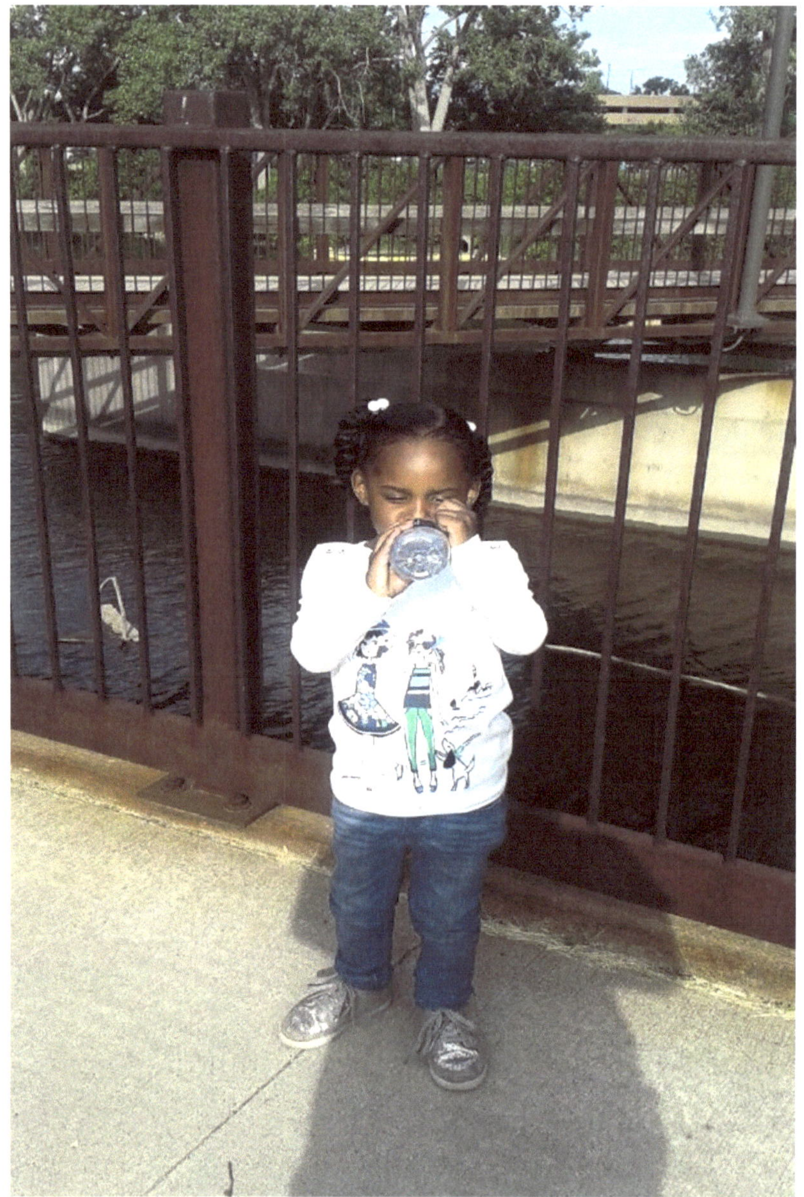

Photographer Christina Cuba

"What are we going to do with some nasty water?"

– 4 year old Malaya Cuba

There can be no keener revelation of a society's soul than the way in which it treats its children."

--Nelson Mandela, Former President of South Africa

Let us sacrifice our today so that our children can have a better tomorrow

--A. P. J. Abdul Kalam

"Children are likely to live up to what you believe of them."

--Lady Bird Johnson, Former First Lady of the United States

"Children are not things to be molded, but are people to be unfolded."

--Jess Lair, author

Each day of our lives we make deposits in the memory banks of our children."

--Charles R. Swindoll, Evangelical Christian Pastor

3 YEAR OLD AUTHOR ANTHONY ELIJAH CAREY

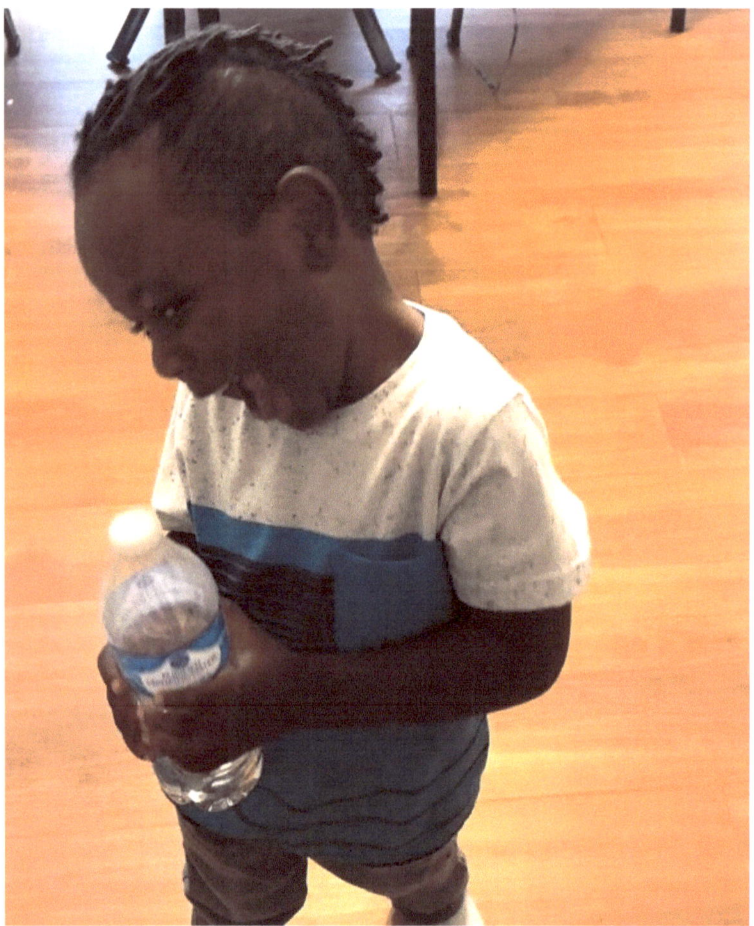

Photo courtesy of Alicia Carey

3-year-old Author Anthony Carey has been taught not to use the water in Flint, Michigan and when visiting a friend's home we pointed to the faucet and little Anthony replied, **"Uh nasty."** Even at age 3, Anthony can tell the impact that the Flint Water Crisis has had on his hometown and how it has changed his behavior and others like him.

--Author Gale Glover

"It is easier to build strong children than to repair broken men."

--Frederick Douglass, abolitionist and statesman

“Children must be taught how to think, not what to think."

--Margaret Mead, cultural anthropologist

"The greatest legacy one can pass on to one's children and grandchildren is not money or other material things accumulated in one's life, but rather a legacy of character and faith."

--Billy Graham, evangelist

"We worry about what a child will become tomorrow, yet we forget that he is someone today."

--Stacia Tauscher, dancer and artist

WHERE ARE THE CHILDREN?

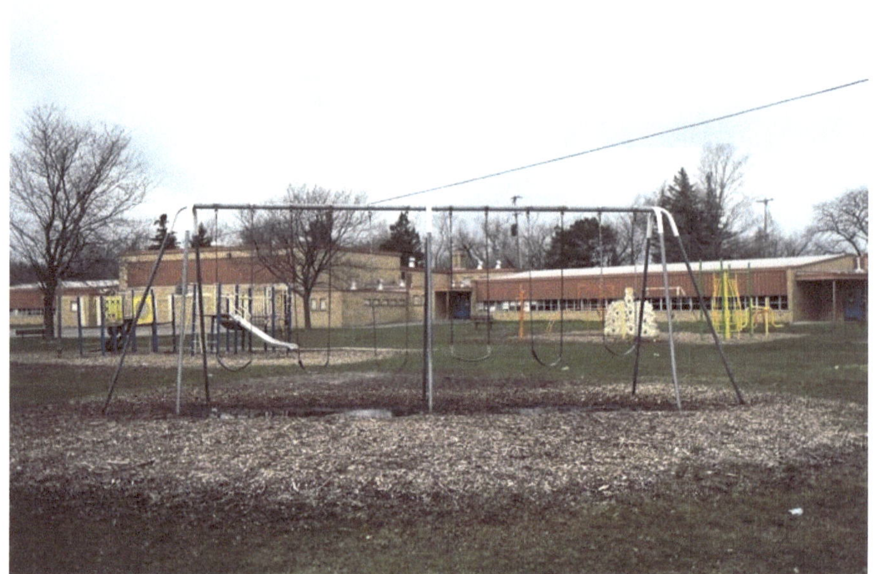

Photographer Jim Cheek

The empty playground represents the children that were affected by lead due to Flint's water contamination source. Many of the children may be unable to play due to the lead poisoning which causes extreme fatigue. Some may be visiting the physician's office or the free lead testing site getting tested for lead. However, another unimaginable theory is that the children may have died from lead poisoning.

We just don't know how many unexplained deaths are a result of the Flint Water Crisis including children. Most recently there has been mention of a possible link between the Flint Water Crisis and the 2015 death of 43 babies all under the age of one. In a July 10, 2017, interview aired by ABC 12 News, Genesee County Health Department worker Mark Valacak voiced the concern of the possible connection. However, the investigation is still ongoing and more evidence is needed to substantiate the claim. So can you tell me?
WHERE ARE THE CHILDREN?

–Author Gale Glover

OUR LITTLE HEROES

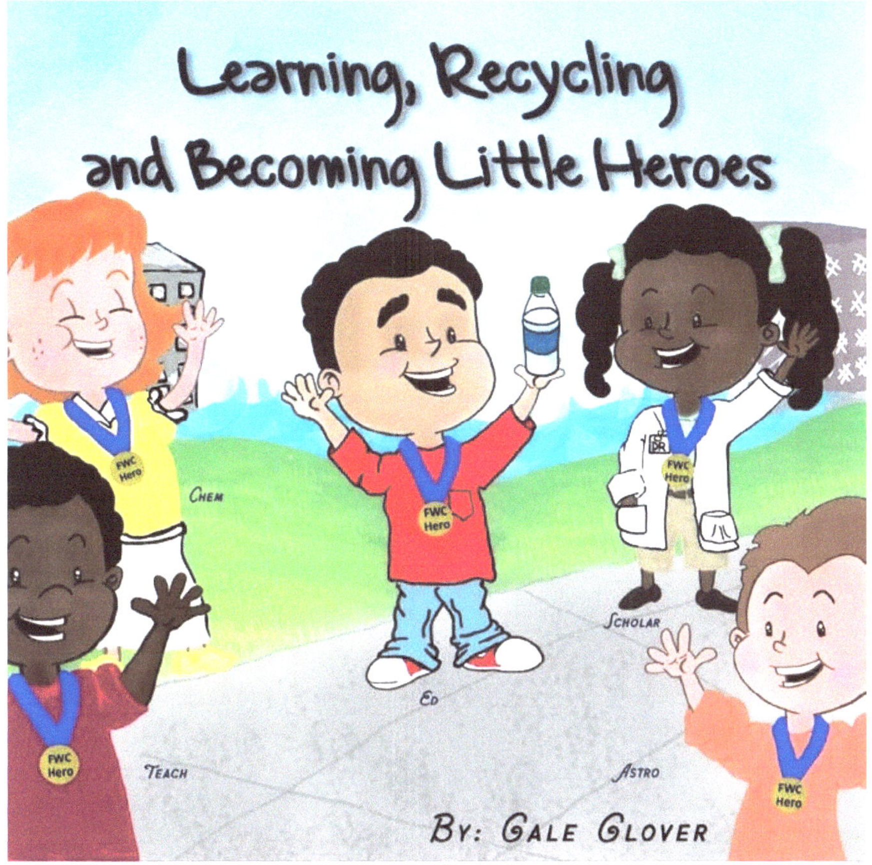

This book pays tribute to the children of Flint, Michigan who had to learn a new way to eat, drink, and live during the Flint Water Crisis (FWC). They are the true FWC heroes, and despite their cities setback many have volunteered hours of their time to pass out water, recycle bottles, and help our community get through this. Children as young as ages 4 and up have volunteered to help pass out water to the Flint residents. Therefore, to the children of Flint, we thank you, we salute you and we award you with the FWC Medal of Honor for being our little heroes.

--Author Gale Glover

www.amazon.com/author/galeglover

JANICE MCCOY
UM-Flint Art Student

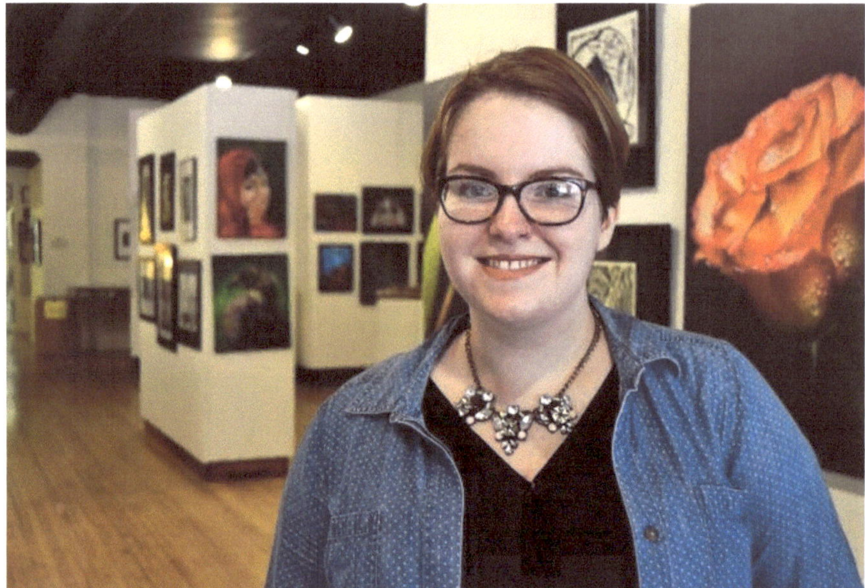

Photographer Amy Hartwig Photo courtesy of Janice McCoy

Janice McCoy is a fine artist, education student and a graphic designer for the School of Management at the University of Michigan-Flint. She is currently pursuing two degrees, a Bachelor of Science in Visual Art Education and a Bachelor of Fine Arts in General Studio Art with a concentration in painting and a minor in Art History at the University of Michigan-Flint. She is a member of the University of Michigan-Flint Honors Program and is working towards finishing her undergraduate thesis, which focuses on the potential of arts education to help struggling students and school districts. Janice exhibits her fine art frequently in the Flint area and is the recipient of multiple awards and scholarships, including the Michigan Scholar full tuition and books (2012-2016), Duesberry Scholarship (2016-2018), consecutive Patty Morello Memorial Award recipient for outstanding art education student (2014-2015, 2017), Overall Outstanding Achievement in Fine Arts (2016) and Exceptional Merit for the 2016 University of Michigan-Flint annual exhibition. She is currently working towards her BFA solo gallery exhibition, which is scheduled for mid-February. Janice lives in Flint, Michigan.

RUSHING WATER

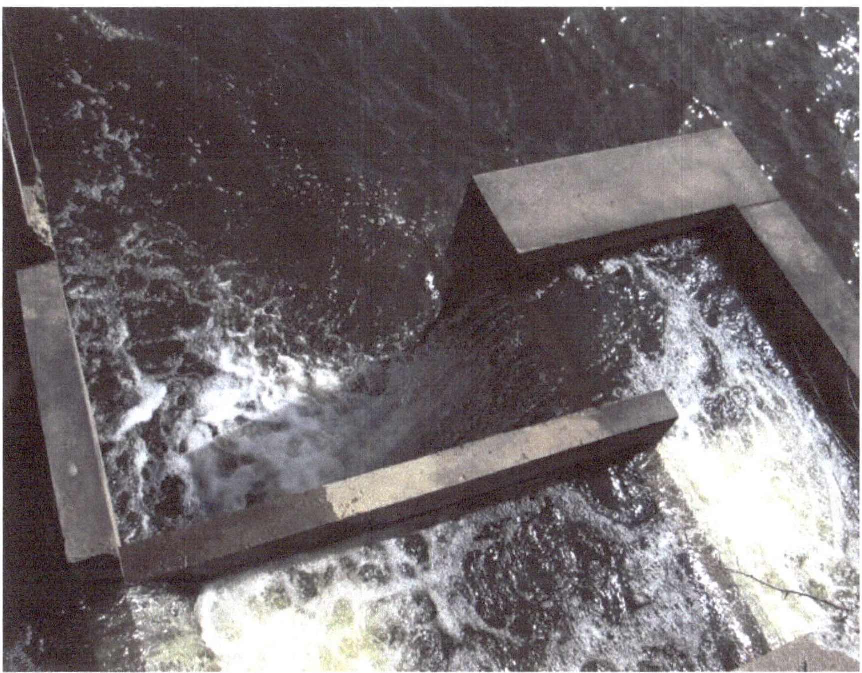

Photographer Janice McCoy

Even before the water crisis, I have always been drawn to the river. Since moving to Flint, it has been one of the most fascinating landmarks that I have been able to discover. Throughout the years, I have spent hours studying it. Dozens of pictures of it sit in my camera and computer memory. I watch it surge through the Hamilton Dam. I watch locals fishing and strolling along its banks. I watch the ice patterns form and then melt. I watch the wildlife and garbage dance across the surface. And it's not because I find it obviously beautiful or picturesque. There are few people who would describe the stretch of the Flint River that winds through downtown as aesthetically pleasing. Nonetheless, I admire the river's movement and power as it rushes along its path. I admire the structures created both to control the river's flow and to traverse its width, despite their obvious age and deterioration. To me, they are symbols of human ingenuity and ability to shape the environment. Historically, the way that cities interact with their surrounding water source is usually quite significant. Rivers are indispensable sources for transportation, drinking, energy, agriculture and more. Therefore, many people would agree that the way a society is able to effectively harness and use a river affects their success. When looking at the Flint River, I can see quite a bit about history, success and failure.

During the last couple of years, as we began to see more and more the extent and ramifications of what was going on with the water system, I struggled to make sense of all of it. As a student, and as someone who did not grow up in Flint, I know that my understanding of the situation is inherently different than someone who has lived here for decades and must continue to do so indefinitely. How do we understand such a tragic and ridiculous event? How do we as artists, students and educators respond? How do we contribute to the conversation in a way that is authentic and productive?

So, with all these thoughts in mind, I am able to reflect on my own experiences with water. I grew up in a rural/suburban area, where wells were common. So the idea of paying for water, especially water that is not safe for consumption, is ridiculous to me. Water is a basic human right. Water is a natural resource. When creating "Free Water", I was thinking about the intense irony that in one of the most economically successful and historically powerful civilizations in human history, there's a great number of Americans who simply don't have safe water. Many of them are in Flint, but now there are emerging reports about other infrastructure and water problems across the nation. For something that should be "free", there are definitely people here in Flint who are paying a great deal for it, and I'm not simply referring to money anymore.

FREE WATER

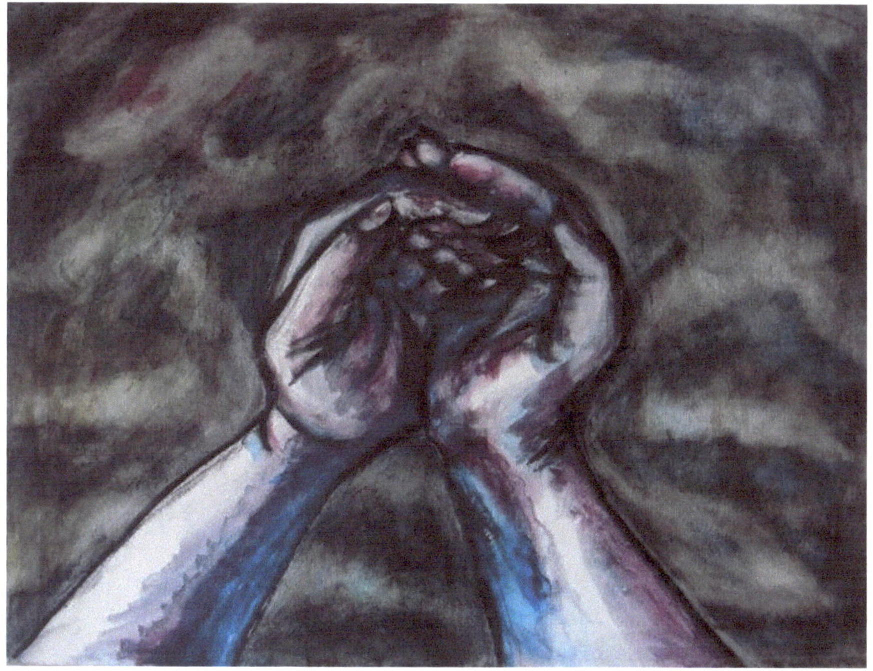

Artwork by Janice McCoy

The Flint Water Crisis cost many people their safety, their children's health and future, their peace of mind and sense of security. It is costing Flint another piece of its already tattered reputation. Finally, it is costing many people their belief in the safety and integrity of our infrastructure and privileges and protections as Americans. My painting is about the common struggles that we all are going to face as we begin to acknowledge environmental problems that are damaging to our health and success as a species.

RAIL EDITS

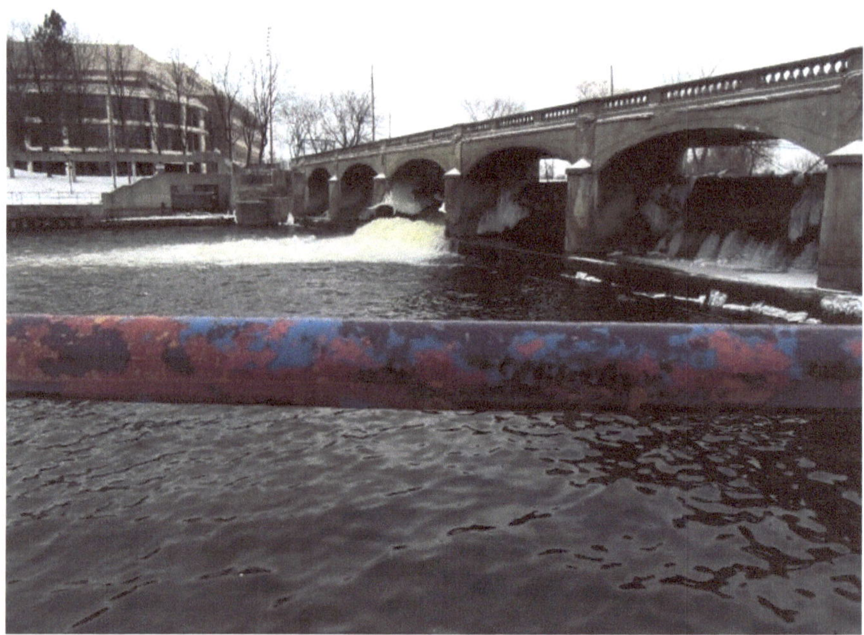

Photographer Janice McCoy

The Flint Water Crisis is something that cannot and will not be forgotten about in the near future. As a student of the University of Michigan-Flint, as a naturalized "Flintstone" and as an artist, I feel an obligation to be a part of the recording of this particular bit of history. If nothing else, I think that people should be reflecting on how we are interacting with and trying to control our environment, and what mistakes we are making. Ultimately we cannot ignore the fact that we are not only destroying natural resources and habitats, but we are also sabotaging our efforts for health and survival. To ensure that we have safe water to drink and clean air to breathe, we have to reflect on where those things originate from and how we can safeguard them for ourselves and future generations.

--Author Janice McCoy

UNDER THE BRIDGE

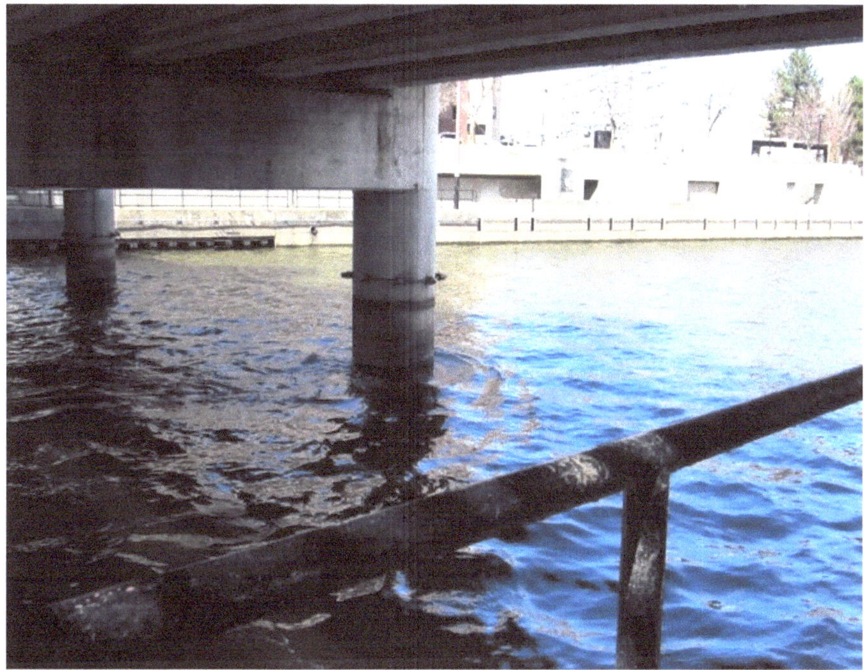

Photographer Janice McCoy

"It is certain, in any case that ignorance, allied with power, is the most ferocious enemy justice can have."

--James A. Baldwin

LEON COLLINS

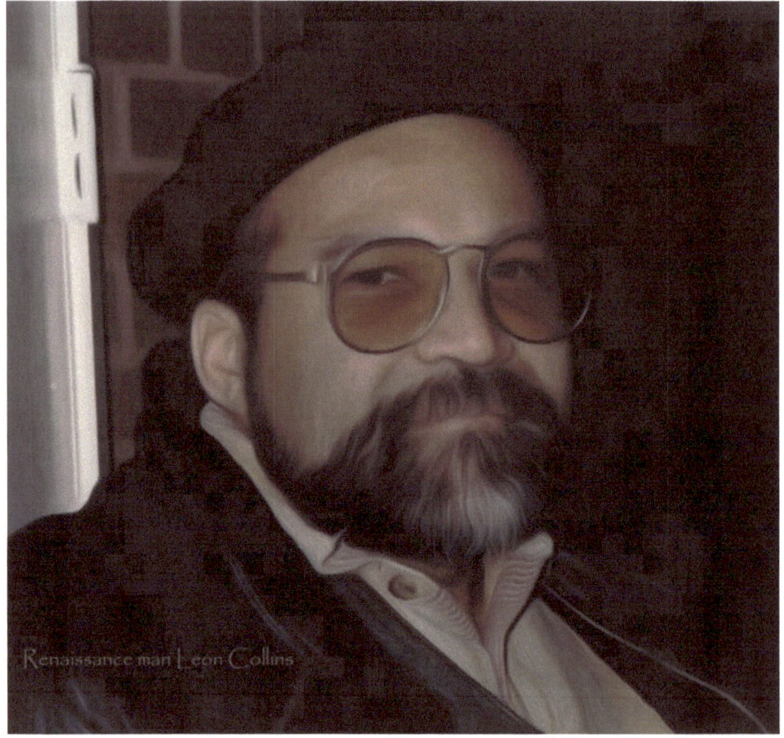

Photo courtesy of Leon Collins

Leon Collins has enjoyed a multi-faceted career path, working in the corporate and nonprofit sectors domestically and internationally as an innovative executive manager, instructor, and educator with experience working in film, community radio, television and T/V. He is co-founder of iMichigan Productions, a 501 (c) (3), startup educational media production company founded by media professionals who are educators.

One of his career highlights was serving as Director of Education and Leadership Programs for the Phelps Stokes Fund one of North America's oldest foundations dedicated to Education for Human Development in the African Diaspora in the Americas, in Africa, indigenous communities in the

Americas and other underserved and marginalized populations.

Earlier in his media career, he was Director of Telecommunications and General Manager for University of Michigan Public Television WFUM TV 28 PBS; Elected Professional Director Public Broadcasting Service (PBS) Board of Directors; Executive Director of Broadcasting University of Houston PBS TV 8; Chairman of the University of Houston's 24 member Distance Learning Taskforce; Executive in Charge of Production BB King and Friends Live at the Woodlands; and Production Consultant/Executive Producer WLII TV Lorimar Telepictures, San Juan, Puerto Rico.

In his work in education, he has been assistant professor of media and communications at Antioch College Center for Social Research and Action in Baltimore, Maryland; consultant to the Washington DC secondary schools, developed a four-year curriculum and instructor for media studies at the Duke Ellington School for the Arts; and media instructor for the George Washington University Workshop for Careers in the Arts. Currently Leon is in the Master of Arts in Arts Administration program at the University of Michigan Rackham School of Graduate Studies with a concentration in the Museum track.

Biography
Leon C. Collins M.A. Arts Administration Management Consultant

"Most organizations are begun by entrepreneurs, grown by leaders, and later optimized by managers." – Roy H. Williams Marketing – The Wizard of Ads

DAMN BARS

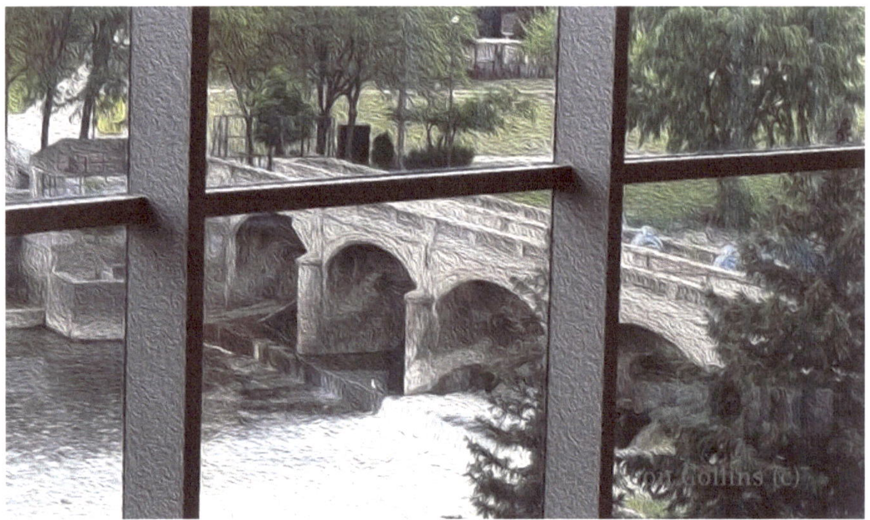

Artwork by Leon Collins

"All the great things are simple, and many can be expressed in a single word: freedom, justice, honor, duty, mercy, hope."
--Winston Churchill

POLLUTION GREEN SLUDGE

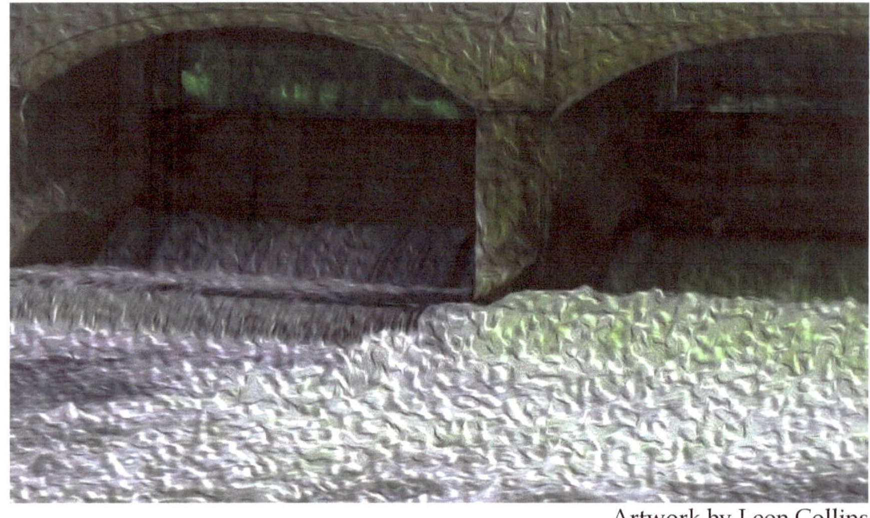

Artwork by Leon Collins

RED DRINKING WATER

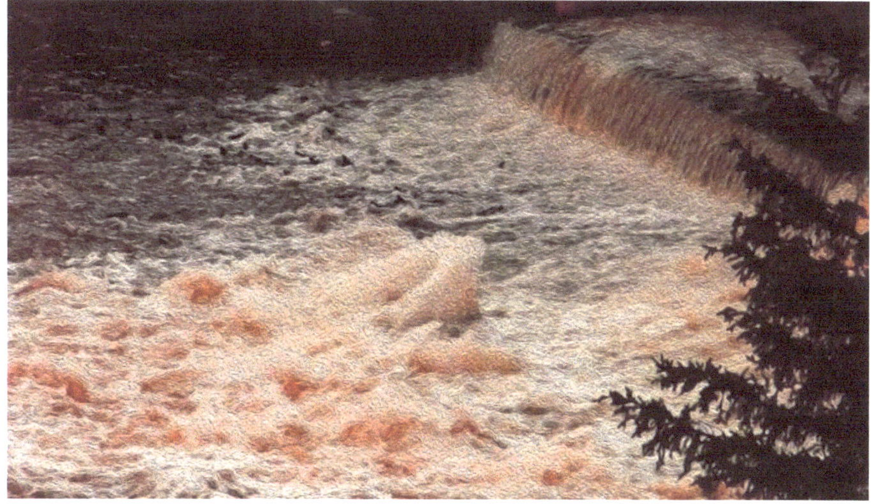

Artwork by Leon Collins

"Law and order exist for the purpose of establishing justice and when they fail in this purpose they become the dangerously structured dams that block the flow of social progress."

--ML King

CONTAMINATION HOPE FOR THE FUTURE

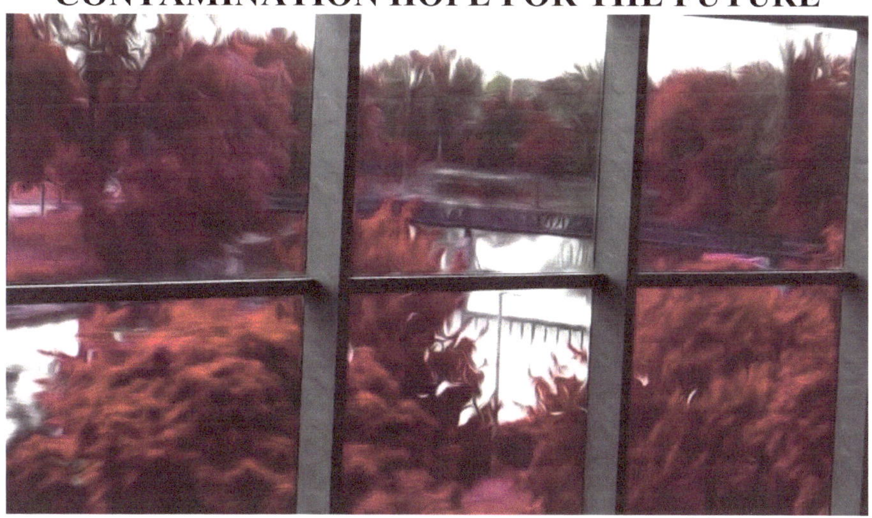

Artwork by Leon Collins

ANIMAL and HUMAN RIGHTS - ASHLEY THORNTON

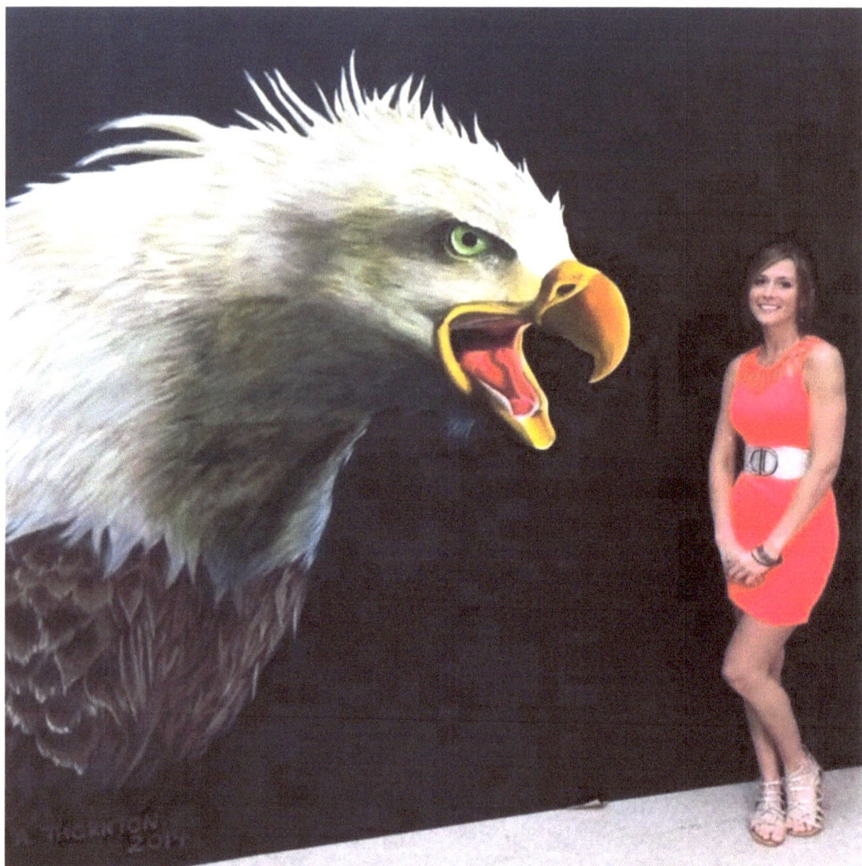

Photographer Aaron Coon | Artwork Ashley Thornton

"With ten years of artist background, Ashley Thornton has focused her skills in photo realistic acrylic paintings. Her talent ranges from the nude to scenery. Although she has a wide range of schooling in all art forms, Ashley prefers to paint animals because of the wide variety of strokes, texture and colors that are involved. Over the years she has shown in local universities, galleries, restaurants and her goal is to expand her works to art markets and more galleries in prominent areas. She graduated with a Bachelor of Fine Arts from the University of Michigan and has a minor in art history. She will continue to explore the acrylic medium while continuing her series of realistic paintings."

PERILOUS WATER

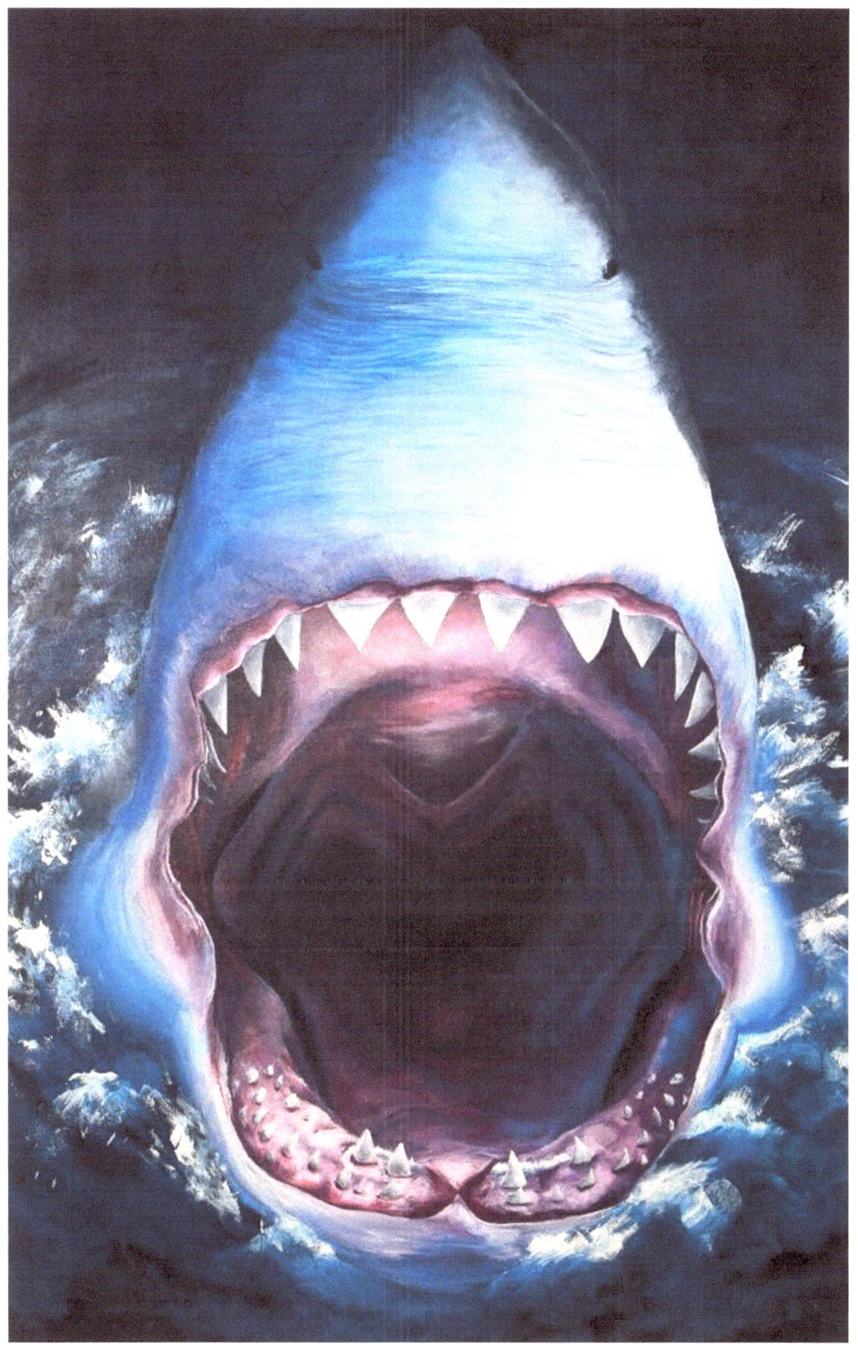

Artwork by Ashley Thornton

The Flint Water Crisis shows a time in history where turbulence, pain, and abuse of power was prominent. Ashley Thornton's painting, "Perilous Water", depicts that struggle. The shark-infested waters of the Flint River coupled with governmental corruption, lead poisoning, and harmful bacteria's running through the pipes of those living in Flint, Michigan. Death was the result and the same can be said if you were attacked by a Shark. However, the sharks, in this case, are not animalistic in the physical sense but those administrative leaders who failed to do their job and protect the residents in the Flint community.

There is another question that we need to examine, that is, how has the Flint Water Crisis affected the animals in the area? In a February 19, 2016, MLive article, Flint Journal reporter Dominic Adams writes, "Four dogs have tested positive for lead poisoning in Genesee County in the last two months, but it is unknown if the animals were in Flint or how they were exposed to the hazardous material." Also, while I, Author Gale Glover was investigating the water crisis, I had numerous reports from Flint residents that their pets have experienced severe hair loss from what they believe was a result of the lead-tainted water. Therefore, it is safe to say that both animal and human rights were violated during the Flint Water Crisis.

--Author Gale Glover

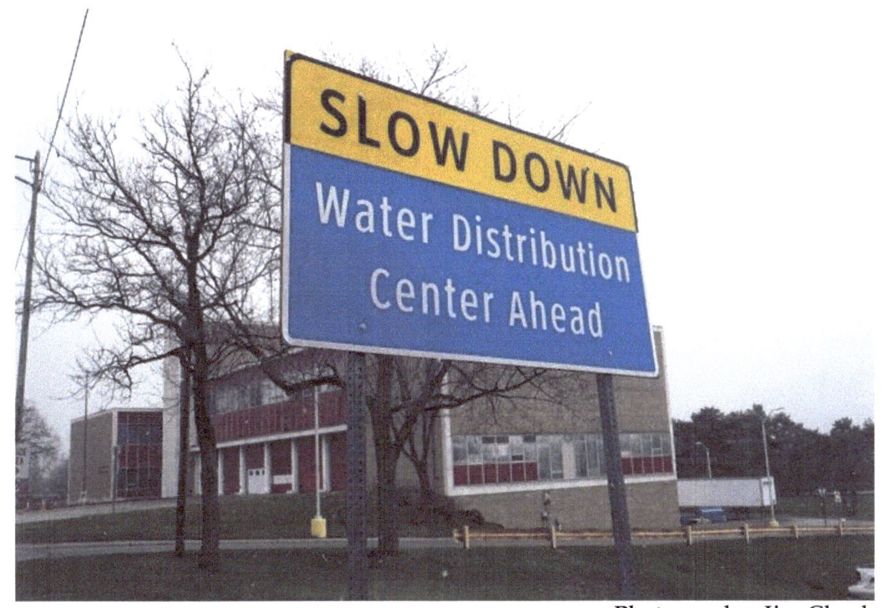

Photographer Jim Cheek

"Water is life, and clean water means health."

- Audrey Hepburn

PAULY M. EVERETT – THE UNDERGROUND KID

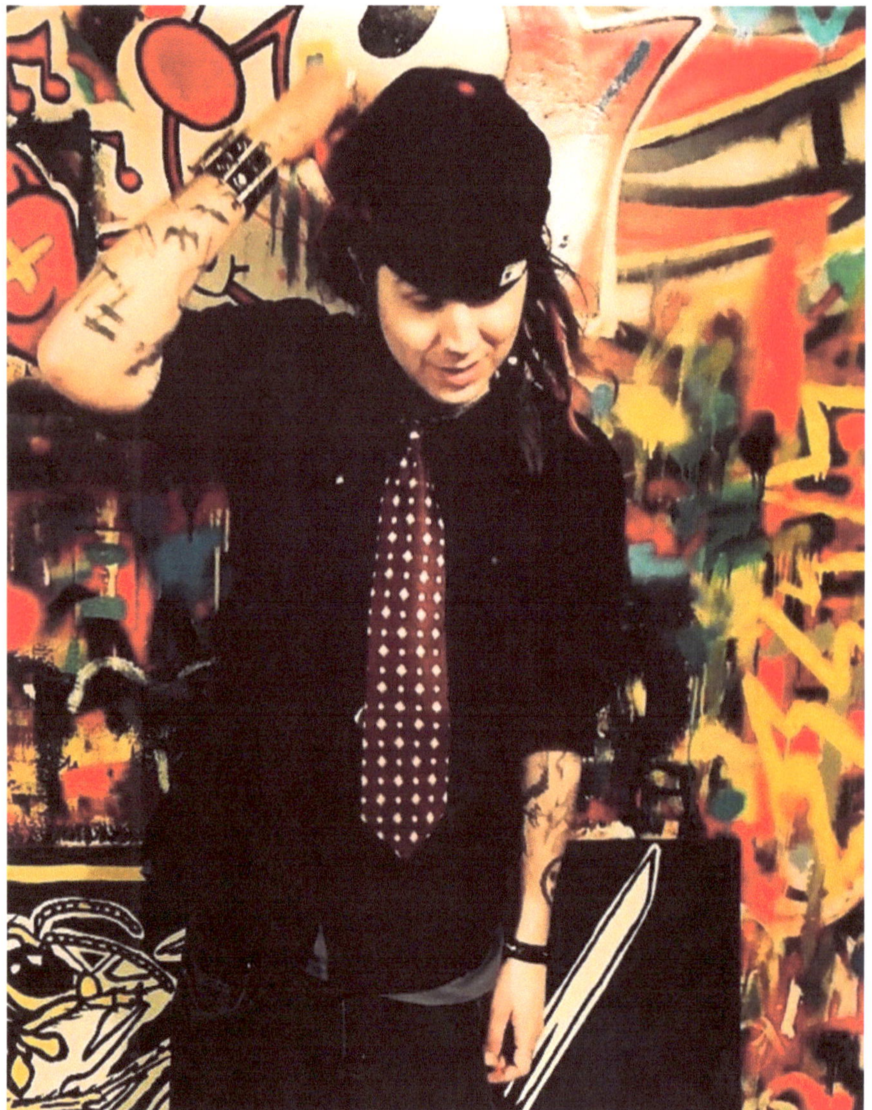

Photo courtesy of Pauly M. Everett

Pauly M. Everett, born in Flint, Michigan, has been involved in the arts since the early years of his childhood. Gaining a solid artistic foundation in his primary and secondary education, he has worked and studied a diverse variety of mixed mediums. Heavily influenced by street art, the underground community, popular culture, music, and travel, he has developed his own career contemporary and abstract style, mixing vibrant color and unique mediums through his painting. Pauly explains his work as "Creating a peaceful experience from the chaotic state that many of us find ourselves sometimes in…"

He enjoys creating works with up-cycled objects such as doors, vinyl records, post-it notes, traffic signs, etc. In his efforts to share an inclusive experience with his community, he engages others, regularly collaborating with fellow artists making art in the streets of Flint and throughout Michigan. He actively promotes and organizes artistic events, focused on growing awareness of the artistic community and empowering creativity within the greater Flint area.

Pauly M. Everett

An Artistic Leader in the Fight for Clean Water

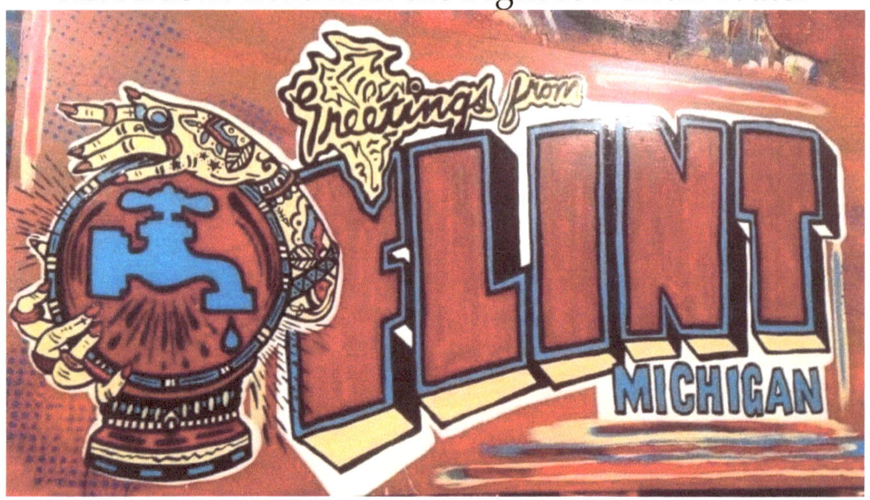

Artwork by Pauly M. Everett

Pauly M. Everett has been instrumental in the fight for clean water, in his hometown of Flint, Michigan. The Underground Kid uses art as a way to express the social injustices plaguing his city. The above artwork depicts a city that is suffering through a contaminated lead water crisis. However, we can see through the use of his colors that Pauly's artwork also portrays a bright future for the city of Flint. Hope, inspiration, and light through a dark tunnel, are beautifully illustrated in his painting. Pauly M. Everett, an artistic leader in the fight for clean water.

--Author Gale Glover

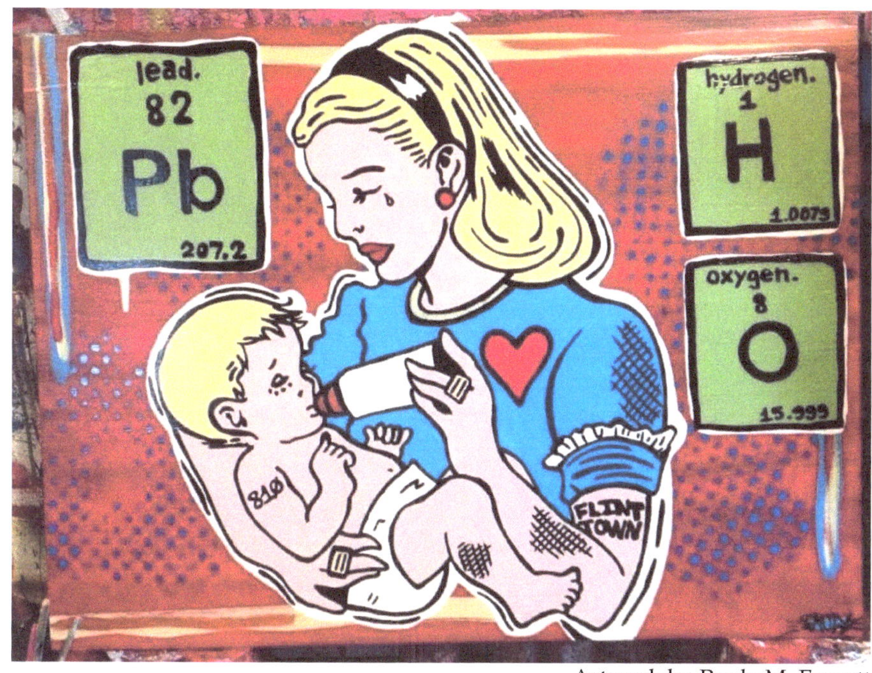

Artwork by Pauly M. Everett

Younger children and fetuses are especially vulnerable to lead because of their developing brains and nervous systems. Decades of research has proven that exposure to even low amounts of lead can affect children's growth, behavior, and intelligence over time. Studies have also linked elevated lead amounts in blood to learning disabilities, problems with attention span, and fine motor coordination and even violent behavior. Pauly M. Everett uses his artistic expression to speak to the wrongs done to the Flint children. Thank you, Pauly!

--Author Katrina Bolton

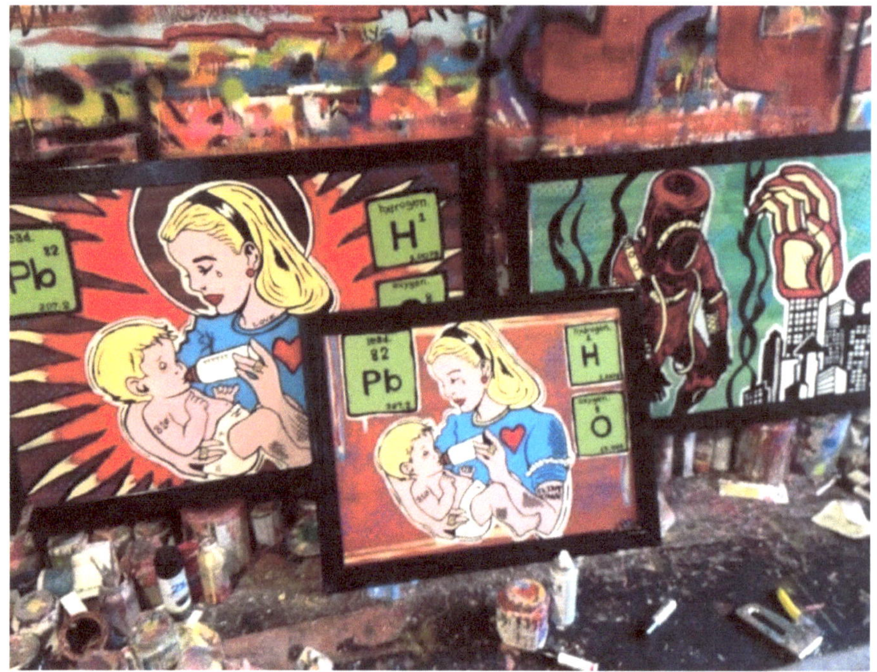

Artwork by Pauly M. Everett

"Throughout history, it has been the **inaction** of those who could have acted, the **indifference** of those who should have known better; the **silence** of the voice of justice when it mattered most; that has made it possible for **evil** to triumph."

--Haile Selassie

TOXICCITY

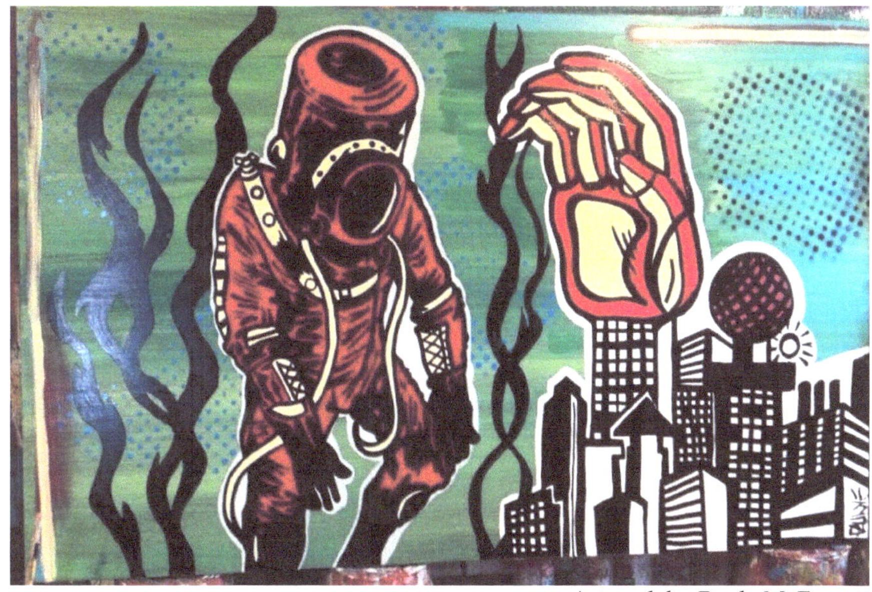

Artwork by Pauly M. Everett

" An area that's as cool as it can get but it's also super toxic and has its problems."

--Pauly M. Everett

"We need to accept the seemingly obvious fact that a toxic environment can make people sick and that no amount of medical intervention can protect us. The health care community must become a powerful political lobby for environmental policy and legislation."

--American Scientist Andrew Weil

PAULY M. EVERETT
A WARRIOR HEART

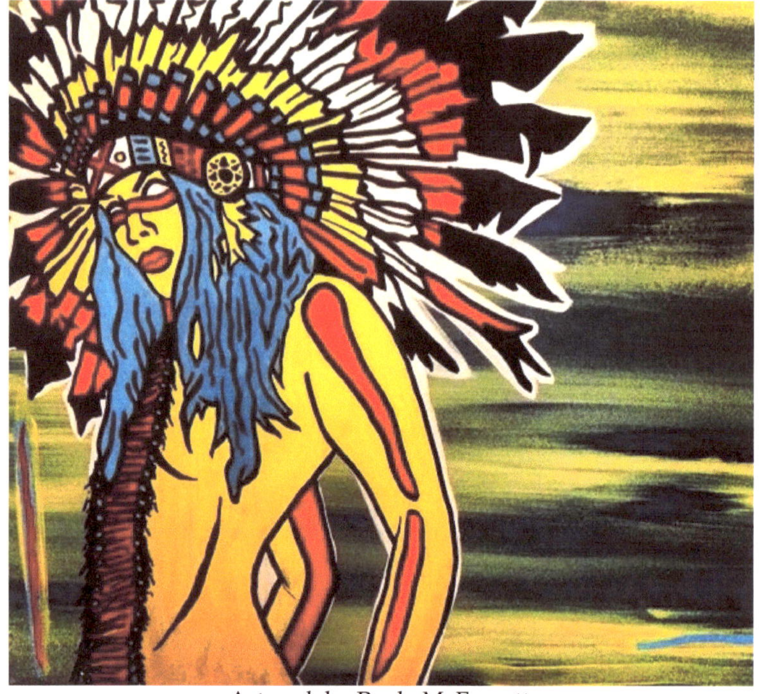

Artwork by Pauly M. Everett

"She's a bit of a reflection of myself. Being a Flint native, you basically have to be ready for whatever, your guard has to be up, and you have to stay consistent in what you do and how you feel, and at the same time open. She's a warrior ready for battle, ready to fight for what she believes in."

--Pauly M. Everett

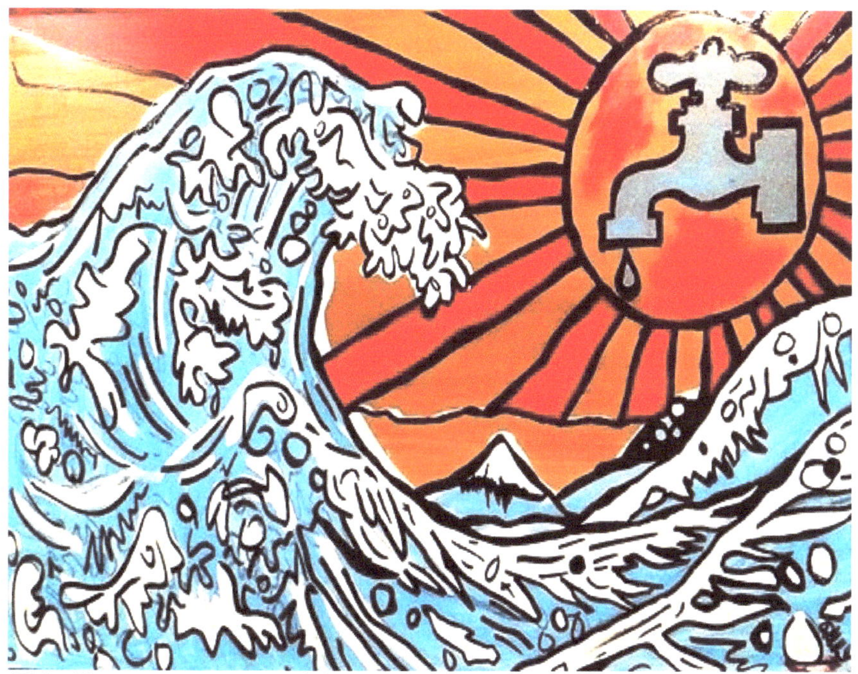

Title: The reinterpretation of the "Great Wave of Kanagawa: by Pauly M. Everett

"From the 1800's the artwork depicts a Tsunami tidal wave which is the cause of many natural disasters. I have always wanted to remix it and going through all of these water issues with fellow natives I figured it would be a good time. Also, most of the art I create is aimed to flip chaos into peaceful, pleasing, and playful creations."

--Pauly M. Everett

AUTHOR AND EVANGELIST KATRINA BOLTON

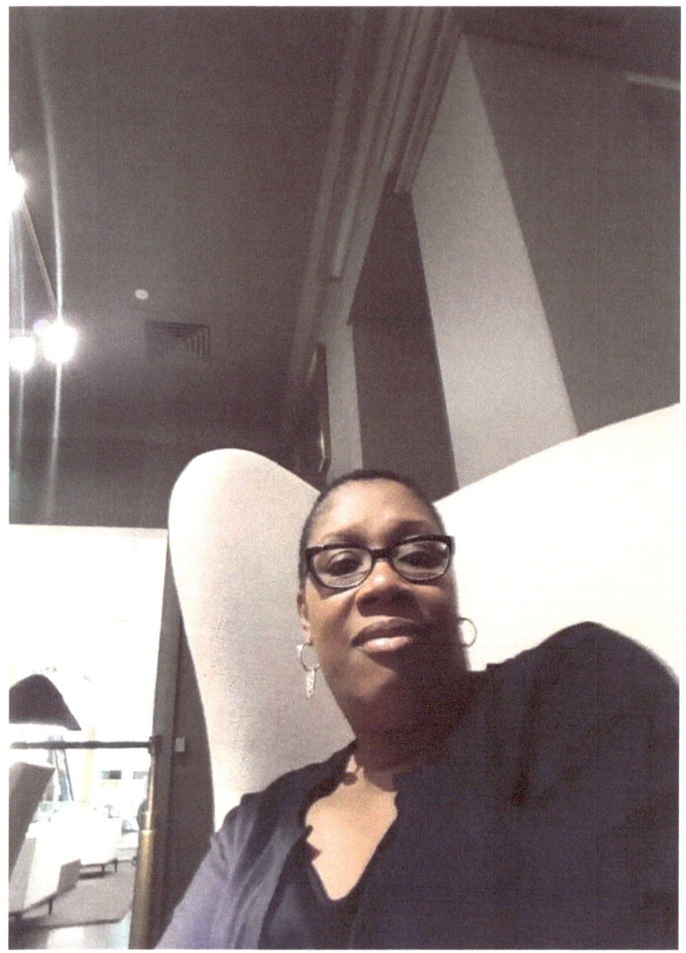

Photo courtesy of Katrina Bolton

Katrina Bolton, is an author, entrepreneur, writer, motivational speaker, and evangelist who loves the Lord, whole-heartedly. She lives her life ministering to all who would listen. It is her belief that there is a Godly purpose for everyone's life and once a person understands their value in society they would thrive within their purpose and be successful. A native of Flint, Michigan. She is touched, sadden and angry by the plague her city is experiencing and have to endure. She enters this project with a heart of compassion and a willingness to give back to the citizen of Flint. May their plight be swift, their scars healed and may they be renewed and restored to fullness of life.
Katrina is a mother of 3 children and grandmother of 10. Learn more about her and her ministry at "Born Selfish", and "Divine Essential Ministries", on Facebook.com and Twitter.com

Katrina is also the owner of LeHorizon Financial Accounting & Business Consulting, LLC, a Christian based company which was established in 2000. The company is responsible for providing outstanding services in the areas of Federal, State and Municipalities Governmental Accounting. It is Katrina's belief that every client who walks through her doors will prosper beyond measure. Katrina stated, "Within our doors we access and forecast the need of our clients, while developing successful strategies for business improvement, grant opportunities and increase profitability. Diligently we work fulfilling all aspects of our clients' Financial, Accounting and Business Consulting needs with dedication and precise accuracy.

We provide the highest degree of confidentiality and integrity. Each client is important and we ensure exceptional Customer's Satisfaction. We are looking forward to meeting with you to discuss your business needs."

THE RIVER, THE FLOW, THE WATER

The River

Dirty, Tainted, Nasty,
Contaminated, unclean,
Unsafe, decay, diseased,
death, destruction, rotten
Lead, lifeless,
Pollution

The Flow

Legionnaires, Cancer,
Corruption, Greed, Deceit, Crime, Murder
Genocide, Inconvenience, Angry
Disgust, Hatred

The Water

Inspirational, free
Safe, clean,
Pure, healing,
Newness,
Life

--Author, Evangelist Katrina Bolton

Sometimes, during a course of our lifetime; we find ourselves in a situation that we haven't foreseen. Needless to say, we are not prepared to handle it. As, in the case of the Flint Water Crisis. No one could have prepared the citizens for the nightmare that they were about to experience. And, until you have lived in that situation no human can comprehend what it is to have your livelihood changed in a winkling of an eye!

I, like many others can only speculate to what it is to have to live daily with using bottle water for your only source of clean water; unless you want to take the risk of getting sick. Imagine a life of living in the City of Flint, Michigan. This is what I perceived a day living in this crisis would be.

A Day without Clean Water

I awaken in the morning and before I can wash my face or my children's face;
I must gather a bottle of water.
Before, I brush my teeth or theirs;
I must gather a bottle of water.
Before, I can bathe myself and my kids;
I must gather several bottles of water and heat the water on the stove.
Before, I can wash my hair;
I must gather bottled water.
Before I can cook a meal;
I must gather bottles of water to wash the meat or cook in.
Before I can wash the dishes;
I must gather bottles of water for washing and rinsing.
Every time, I want a drink or make lemonade;
I must gather a bottle of water.
At the end of the day; I have gathered hundreds of bottles of water
And then I must dispose of them.
And, before I can do any of this……I must go to the distribution center to get more bottles of water!

Author, Evangelist Katrina Bolton

It's Just the Way It is! By Katrina Bolton

Once, she stepped off the bus; she took off running at full speed, into the house. Momma, Momma, Momma; are you here? Momma, where are you? She yelled. In the kitchen, Katie. What's wrong? Did something bad happen at school today? No, nothing bad. I just got something important to tell you. She grazed into her mother's face and smiles. Well, what is it baby girl? Her mother begins to wonder what her child would come up with now.

Well, in school today; a man came to speak to us from the Flint Water Plant. He talked about our water. Momma, it wasn't easy understanding what he was saying. He didn't explain things well. Our class had so many questions for him but, he wouldn't tell us what we wanted to know. He talked about where our water came from and the way it travels to get to our faucets. But, momma we don't get our water from the faucet, our water comes from a bottle. We once got it from there but not now, things have changed. We can't use our water. It's yucky. It's nasty. It's brown and it stinks! When you look at it, it makes your skin crawls and when you drink it, it makes your stomach turns flips.

Momma, the man wouldn't tell why our water is that way, why we must live like this, or how did this happen to us. He only told us how that nasty water travels to get to our kitchen sinks. So, momma, I'm asking you my questions, Why?

Well Katie, someone in our city and state government made a terrible mistake. How momma? Her mother begin to explain. They wanted to save money so, they took our good water away and gave us bad water which was full of lead and other unhealthy things. Baby, that's why our water is brown and full of harmful things. That's why we can't drink it and our water pipes may never be fixed. Little do we know.....we may not never be able to drink it again...But; that's why our lives have changed. And, that's why we got to take baths with bottle water, brush our teeth with bottle water; wash our hair with bottle water; cook our food with bottle water, and wash our dishes with bottle water. That's why our clothes look dim and dirty. That's why we are inconvenienced and must make trips to the water distribution centers. Baby, therefore we suffer and are losing our patience and hope in this devastating situation.

Why would someone do that to us, Momma? Why, Katie, that's a good question. All, I can say is that sometime people who are in politics don't seem to care about the people who they service and are responsible for. They fail to have compassion, sympathy or empathy for others. Sometimes, they think that they know it all and know what best in every situation. Sometimes, they think that what they want to do is all that matters. Rarely, do they ask the people what they want and listen to their opinions. Often, they just do what they think is best for us, without thinking about what the little people has to endure or overcome with their decision makings.

Momma, would we ever get our lives back again and live the way we used to? Katie, I don't know if, that would ever be possible again but for now.......**it's just the way it is!**

--Author, Evangelist Katrina Bolton

DR. TRACI CURRIE
AN ADVOCATE FOR CHANGE

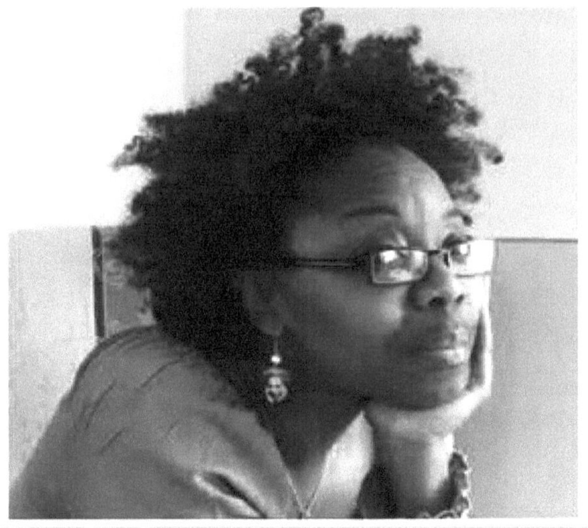

Photo courtesy of Dr. Traci Currie

Traci Currie, Ph.D
Collegiate Lecturer in Communication, University of Michigan-Flint
Education: Ph.D. Media Studies, Ohio University
Emphasis Area: Media Studies
Area of Expertise: Cultural Studies and Identity; Spoken Word Performance
Website: www.tracicurrie.com

Dr. Traci Currie is a community activist who advocates for youth and young adults within the Flint community. Through mentorship, spoken word, and social awareness Dr. Currie creates a safe space for young people to voice their concerns about the problems surrounding their city. Dr. Currie also creates future leaders who will serve to produce a positive change in Flint, a city struggling to recover from a water crisis.

FLINT

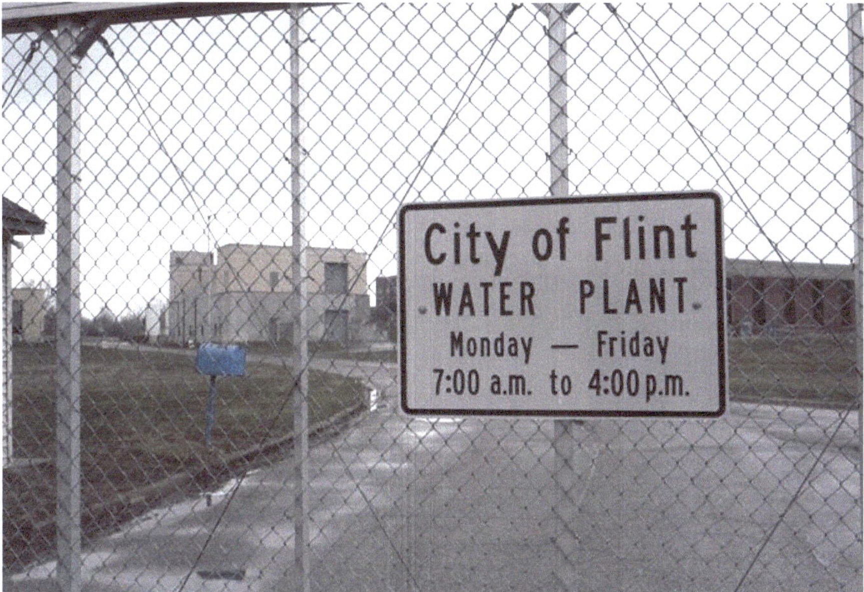

Photographer Jim Cheek

Flint's water crisis symbolically represents the global landscape that we are a part of. In many ways She, Flint, is a humble reminder that people across lands and cultures create their own space of salvation, safety, and survival during disastrous times and circumstances. This poem reflects the hardship of Flint, way past the water crisis. Flint was in the news for other concerns (i.e. crime, education, job loss, housing disparities) before the water contamination hit the airwaves. The water situation compounds an already frustrated environment. The changing season in this short poem serves as a metaphor for how we shift the way we think about the spaces in which we live.

--Dr. Traci Currie

SHE, FLINT

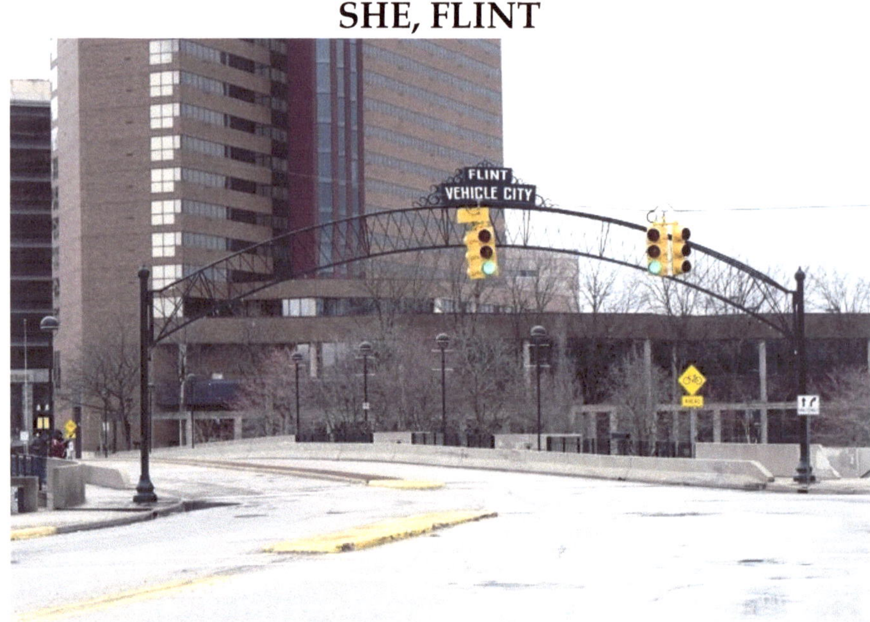

Photographer Jim Cheek

She, Flint
Forever gem
calls to me in cold-to-warm season
broken paved roads
hole induced
winter worn
closing shops early because she sleeps
even if people do not.

Depressed in unlit areas
Calling on vitamin d
while zombie-angst spirits
ride lull buses
living to complain
because it is easiest
in this unspoken gem.

Weather shifts

green comes
gardens rear their heads in her earth
art walks 2nd Friday of the month all year
but art actually walks in warmer seasons
abc12 lettering itself to z
localizing the whereabouts
for gm townies
home is a base
to build again
breathe again
brave familial grounds
and fall in love with
Forever gem
again.

--Dr. Traci Currie

FLINT SONGBIRD
CARRIE RILEY

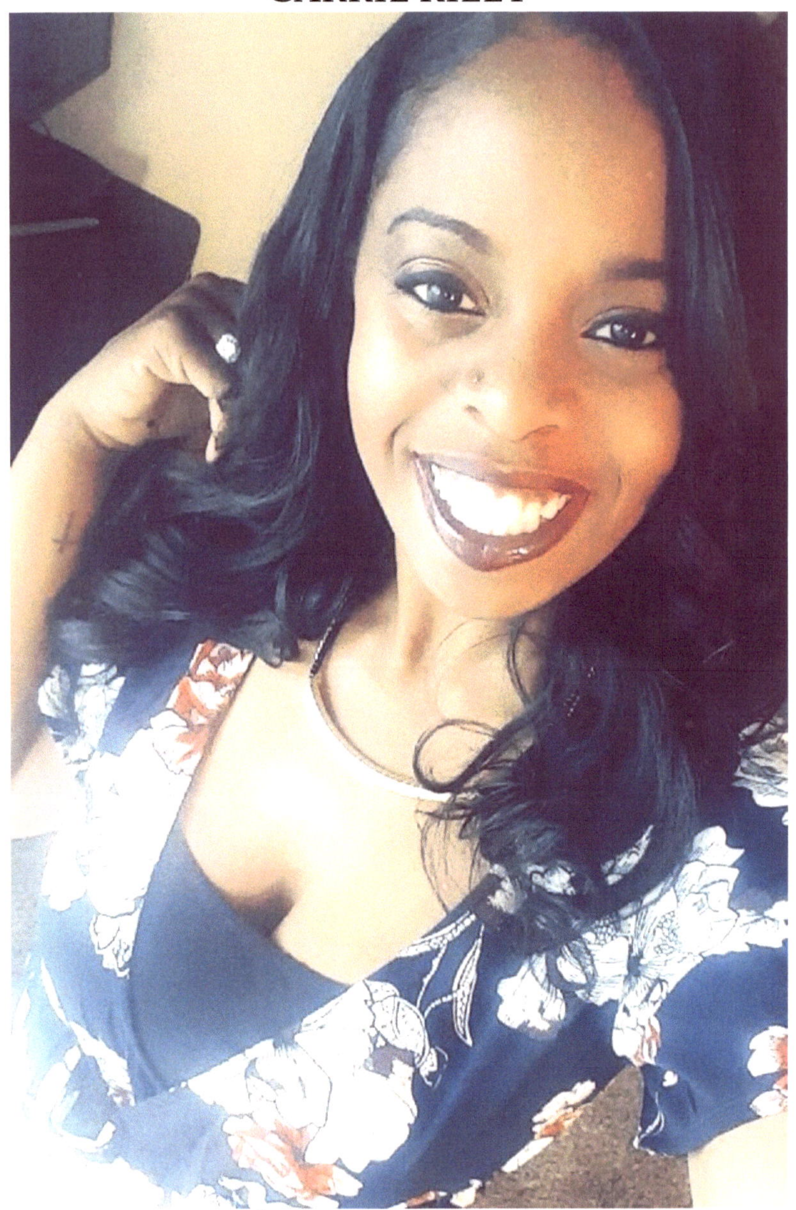

Photo courtesy of Carrie Riley

THE REAL CRISIS

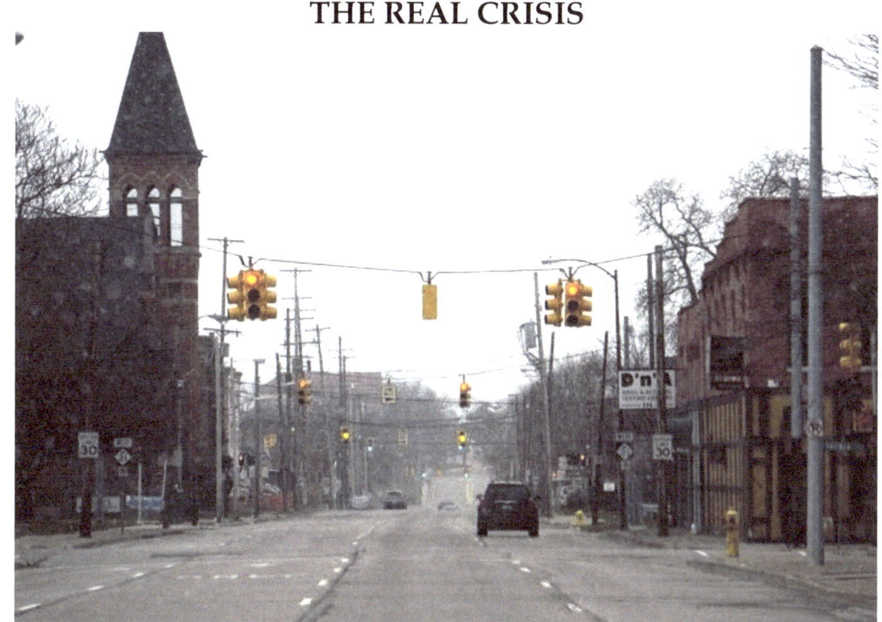

Photographer Jim Cheek

Unveiling the truth in a dark place
Our city, our home, our only space
Murders rates are through the roof
The stress of paying for necessities, that could easily kill you
Leaders with power, though it seems nobody cares
We need assistance don't believe everything you hear
We just don't want our children to live in fear
A simple bath or brushing your teeth
Could lead to death pain and misery
Without even the basics, how can one be safe
We just need help to pick up the pace
Help us save our city & redistribute the peace
Flint, our city, our home, our only space

--Author Carrie Riley

CHRISTINA CUBA

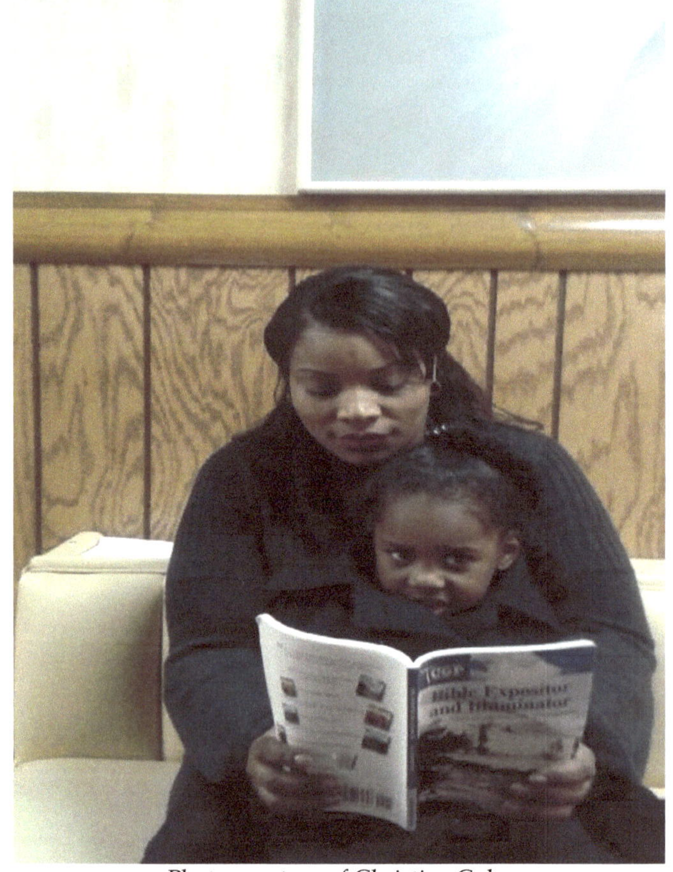

Photo courtesy of Christina Cuba

Christina Cuba was born in Flint, MI but raised in Wetumpka Alabama. She returned to Flint and earned an Associate's Degree in Visual Communications and is currently a candidate for her Bachelors in Visual Communications at the University of Michigan-Flint. She is also the church secretary and Sunday school teacher at Joy Missionary Baptist Church and wants to inspire others to live creatively.

A MOTHER'S SORROW

Mother Christina Cuba is seen reading to her 4-year-old daughter Malaya Cuba. However, during the last three years, things have changed. Malaya was just one of many children exposed to high amounts of lead due to the Flint Water Crisis. Mom Christina stated that "We were told that the water was fine after a while so we've had lead hotdogs and we've had lead oatmeal and it came to a point where Malaya said she didn't want her food and I was wondering why she didn't want to eat. Then when they said we found out that the water still wasn't good, I realized it was the Lord telling me not to give my daughter this food or make her eat it. Even though I believe that you should eat all your food and you shouldn't waste anything but I don't want to kill her." Just like many of the parents in Flint, Michigan Christina felt the anguish of knowing that her child was given lead-contaminated food.

Christina and her only child Malaya Cuba are also featured in the upcoming book Flint the Death and Rebirth of a City. Christina is an illustrator, author and muralist painter and she hopes that by sharing her story it will inspire others to speak out against any injustice, against any man, woman, or child.

--Author Gale Glover

ARTISTS TREADING WATER EXHIBIT

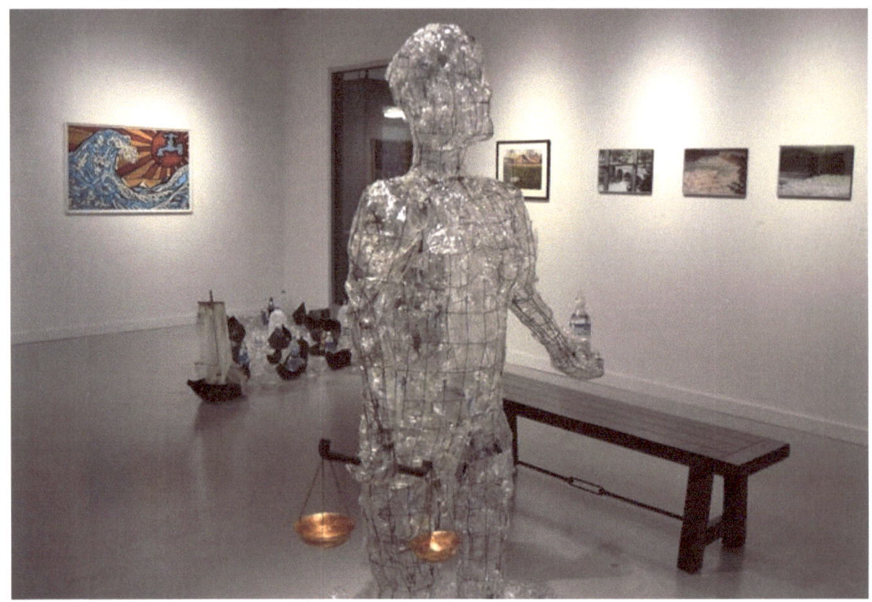

Photographer Amy Hartwig

Photographer Amy Hartwig was able to capture the true essence of the Artist Treading Water exhibit created by the University of Michigan-Flint faculty, staff, and students in partnership with Mott Community College and local artists. The depiction shows artwork by The Underground Kid Pauly M. Everett, Dr. Jjenna Hupp Andrews, The Renaissance Man Leon Collins, and Photographer Jim Cheek.

--Author Gale Glover

ARTISTS TREADING WATER EXHIBIT

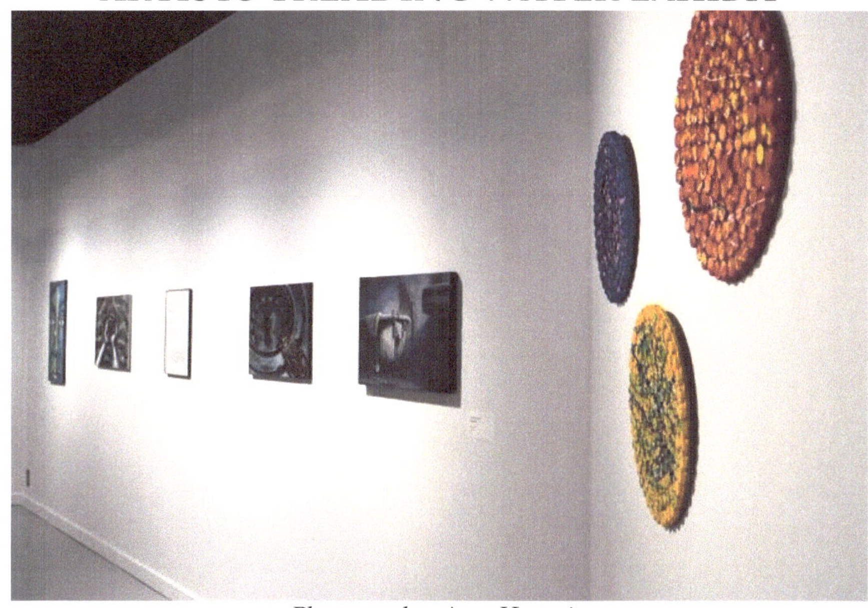

Photographer Amy Hartwig

This picture also depicts the artwork created to bring awareness to the Flint water crisis. The photo was taken by Photographer Amy Hartwig. The beautifully designed artwork is by Dr. Traci Currie, Rhonda Jones, Robert Downer, Janice McCoy, and Criss Kelly.

--Author Gale Glover

ROBERT DOWNER
UNIVERSITY OF MICHIGAN – FLINT ALUMNI & GRADUATE STUDENT

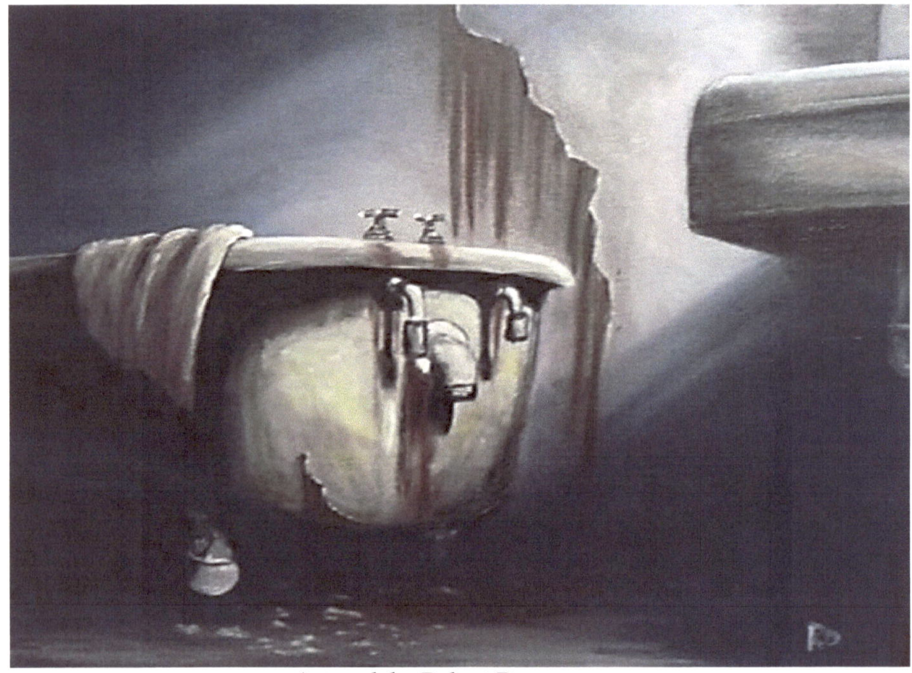

Artwork by Robert Downer

University of Michigan-Flint Alumni and current graduate student Robert Downer received his creativity from his dad who practiced wood carving. All three pieces by Robert titled Bathtub, Window, and Sink shows the acid like, lead-tainted water destroying the structure of a Flint home.

--Author Gale Glover

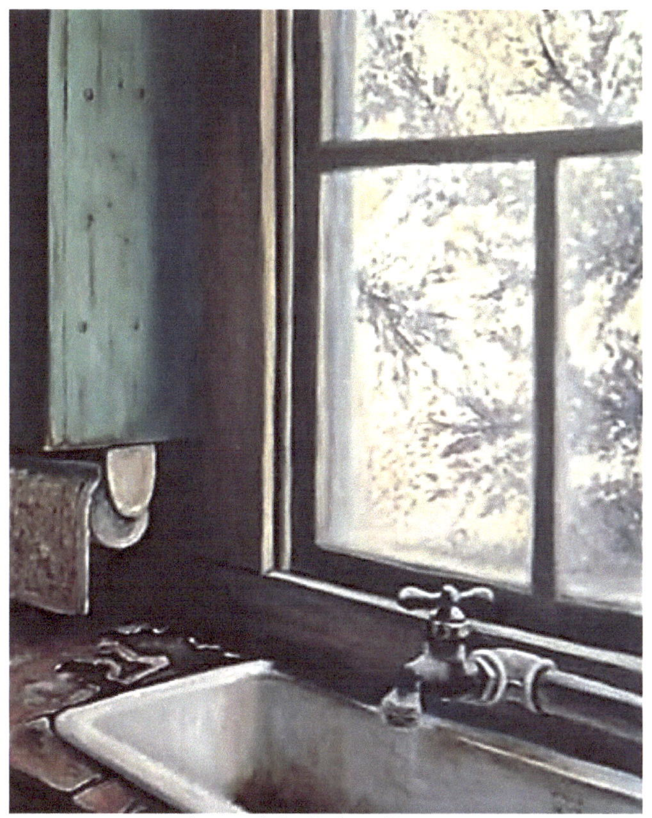

Artwork by Robert Downer

"Until justice is blind to color, until education is unaware of race, until opportunity is unconcerned with the color of men's skins, emancipation will be a proclamation but not a face."

--Lyndon B. Johnson

"**Law and order** exist for the purpose of establishing **justice** and when they **fail** in this purpose they become the dangerously structured dams that block the flow of **social progress.**"

--ML King

“Pollution of water…is killing more children today than malaria or AIDS or even wars themselves.”

--Tony Clarke

RHONDA JONES
UNIVERSITY OF MICHIGAN-FLINT ALUMNI

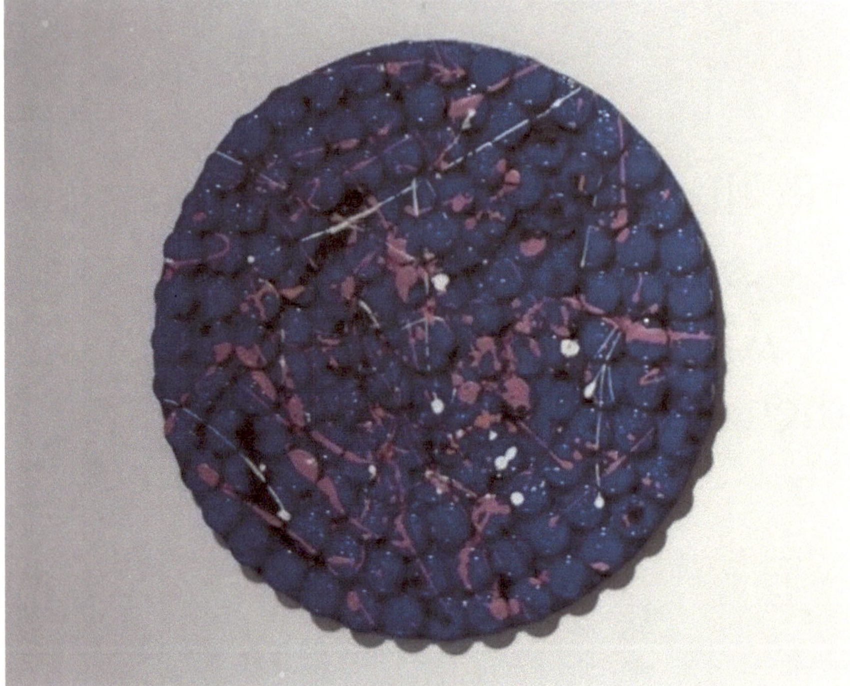

Artwork by Rhonda Jones

The above mural was created by University of Michigan-Flint Alumni Rhonda Jones. The mural was made from water bottle caps that Rhonda collected and was an artistic way to encourage recycling while bringing awareness to the Flint Water Crisis.

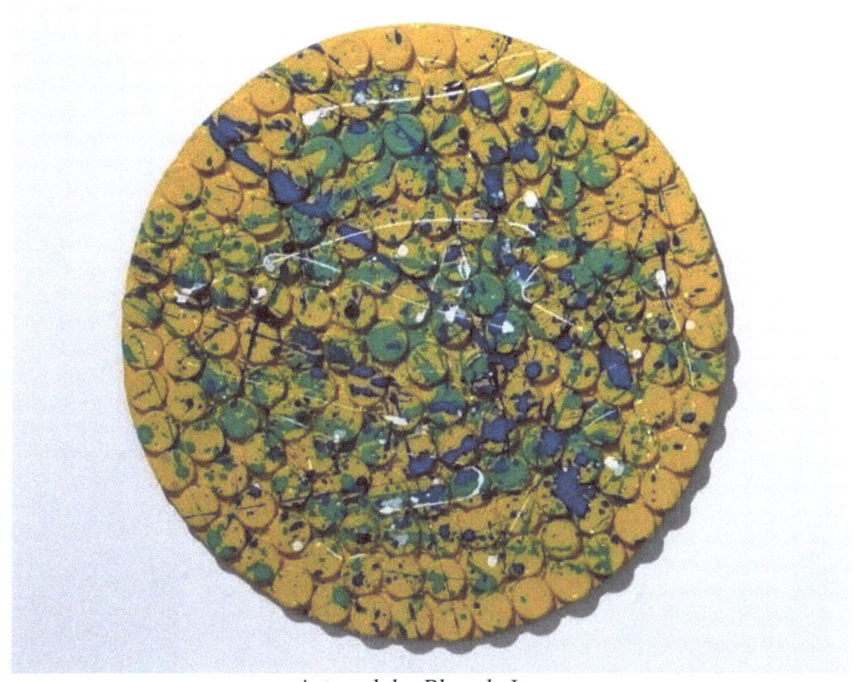
Artwork by Rhonda Jones

"The moral arc of the universe bends at the elbow of justice."

--ML King

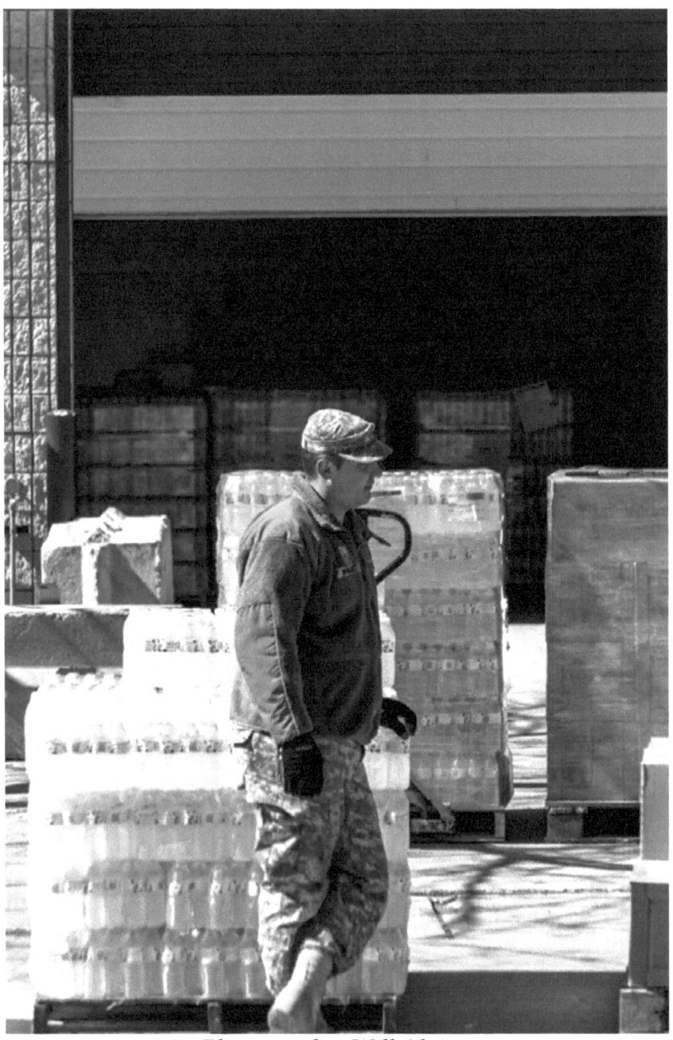

Photographer Will Alston

Photographer Will Alston captures the moments of the National Guard who were dispatched to institute a water distribution site. Will states, "I don't live in Flint but I am a University of Michigan-Flint student and I was affected by the flagrant bias of government actions towards a certain population of people based on race and socioeconomic status."

--Author Gale Glover

PHOTOGRAPHER WILL ALSTON

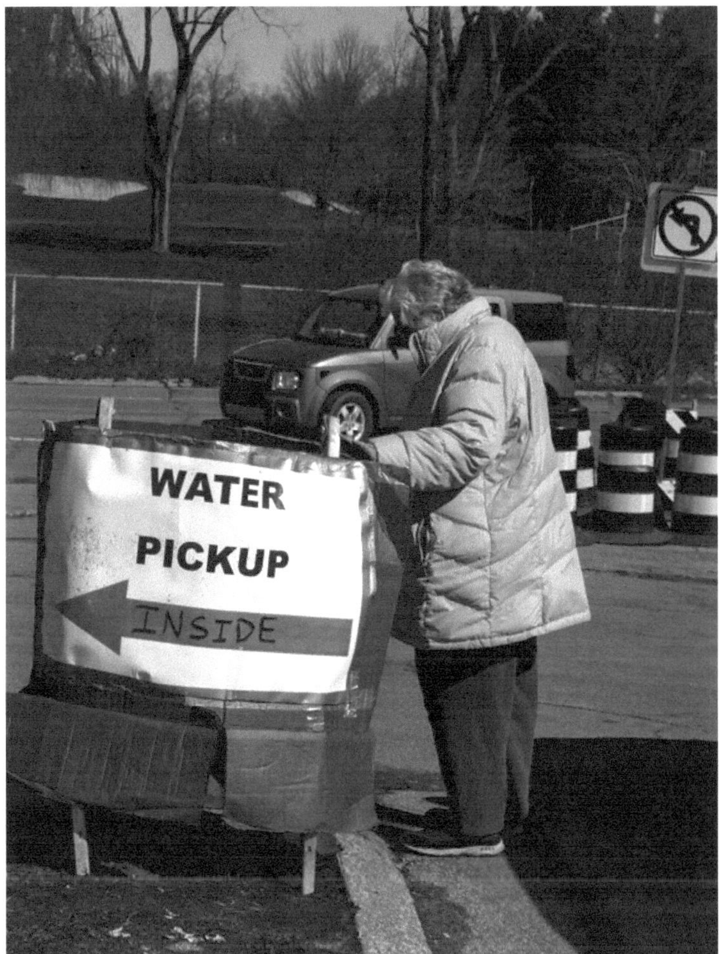

Photographer Will Alston

"We've poisoned the air, the water, and the land. In our passion to control nature, things have gone out of control. Progress from now on has to mean something different. We're running out of resources and we are running out of time."

~ **Robert Redford**

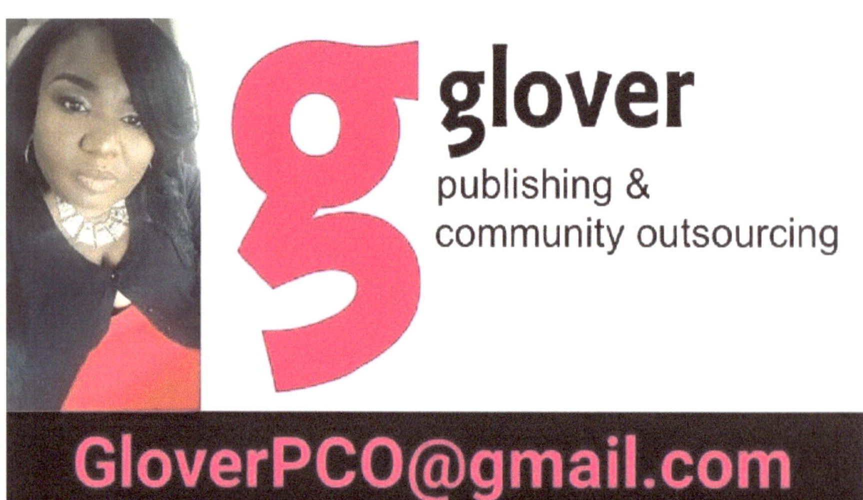

Gale Glover, a native of Flint, Michigan has become an iconic figure in the Flint community. She holds a Bachelor of Arts in Criminal Justice, Sociology, and Africana Studies, a Master's in Public Administration, and a post-masters education specialist degree with a superintendent administrative certification. Her goal is to also pursue a doctorate in education so that she may help others achieve their educational goals.

Gale is an established author and has written seven books with three upcoming books. Her children's book "Learning, Recycling, and Becoming Little Heroes", depicts the strength of the Flint children during the water crisis. In addition, her "Reach Higher Ed Series" helps kids get prepared for higher education. Gale noted the importance of higher education by stating, "It's important to get kids thinking about college earlier so they can successfully complete it in a more affordable manner."

To add to her many accomplishments, Gale has started a nonprofit called, "Flint Kids Matter" which focuses on improving literacy, getting kids prepared for higher education, developing workforce skills, and recovering from the effects of the Flint Water Crisis. A percentage of the water crisis books goes to help fund Flint Kids Matter and provides book donations for children. Gale has also been recognized as ABC News Person of the Week and has been nominated for the Christ Enrichment Literacy Award. Those are just a few of her many accomplishments, but her passion to empower, educate and enrich the lives of people within her community supersedes her reputation.

Like many kids in Flint, Gale grew up in a single parent household, mother no father and she is the younger of two siblings. Growing up poor, Gale also struggled with literacy so it is easy for her to relate to kids in similar situations. Gale is a survivor of domestic abuse and has conquered many obstacles in her life. Her passion comes from that pain and compels her to help others reach their goals. Gale has a strong faith and believes that through God, along with persistence and prayer, you can achieve anything. Gale went on to start her own publishing company and hires many local artists to work alongside her. Her dedication to the Flint community is unparalleled. Gale Glover, Flint Born! Flint Bred! Flint Educated!

To purchase any of her books please visit www.amazon.com/author/galelgover

FLINT - GENOCIDE

In 1948, in Guatemala,
The government infected the soldiers
1300 people some of which died
All because the government lied
It was genocide

In 2014, in Flint, Michigan
The government infected the water
Similar to Guatemala
A governmental experimentation
An assassination
And the elimination
Of a city, demeaned by a nation

Governmental officials, we got the hint
Of the contamination that you sent
Of all the Flint Residents
And we still have to pay water and rent
It just don't make sense

In 1948, in Guatemala, the government infected the soldiers
And in 2014, in Flint, Michigan, the government wanted to get rid of them
So they repeated Guatemala and infected again
Lead, L E A D stands for Let Every Adolescent Die
And what the government did for the 2nd time
It was genocide

--Author Gale Glover

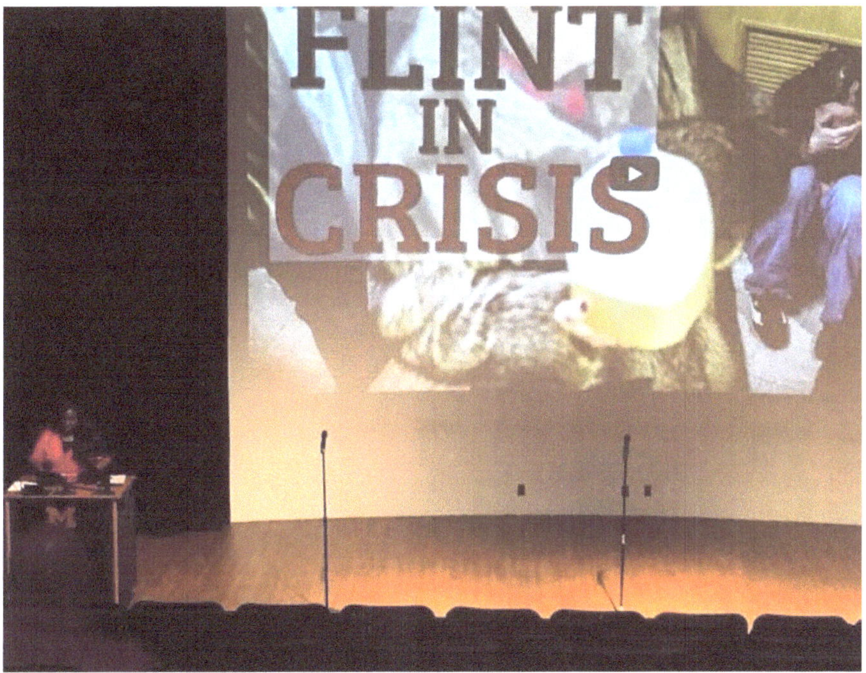

Photo courtesy of Gale Glover Photographer Chris Waters

Author Gale Glover recites her poem "Flint Genocide" at the Artists Treading Water Exhibit held at the University of Michigan - Flint.

Flint is still recovering so we need your help. For more information please contact FlintKidsMatter@gmail.com

COMING MARCH 2018

www.amazon.com/author/galeglover

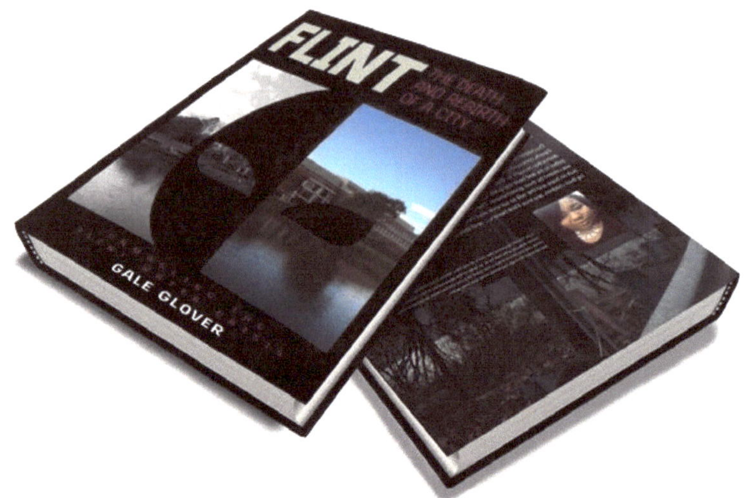

Photographer and Illustrator Jacob Johnson

Gale Glover, Author of Flint: The Death and Rebirth of a City wrote this book to bring awareness to what happened in Flint, Michigan and to make sure that no one ever forgets. The Flint Water Crisis marked the destruction of an infrastructure and the poisoning of a city which included men, women, and most importantly children. This book illustrates two sides to that story, the Death which includes genocide and the creation of the Apocalypse: Disease, Death, Strife, and Famine.

Then there is the Rebirth which some say does not exist however, this book is proof of that rebirth. People banding together to create social change using their voice to fight against the destruction created by their government. Leading protest after protest while creating new organizations to lead in the fight, using artistic expression to tell their Flint Water Crisis story. Standing up to fight in a peaceful manner because that is what the residents of Flint, Michigan were born to do and that you ask is the REBIRTH. **--Author, Gale Glover**

Thank you, for your contribution to this project. May your interpretation of this Crisis be felt in all the hearts of those who are affected the most.

--Authors, Gale Glover and Katrina Bolton

Will Alston
Amy Hartwig
Dr. Jienna Hupp Andrews
Katrina Bolton
Alicia Carey
Anthony Carey
Jim Cheek
Leon Collins
Christiana Cuba
Malaya Cuba
Dr. Tracie Currie
Robert Downer
Pauly M. Everett
Ben Gaydos
Davontae Glenn
Caleb Glover
Gale Glover
Percy Glover
Amy Hartwig
Jacob Johnson
Rhonda Jones
Janice Mc Coy
Kamariya Miller
Carrie Riley
Ashley Thornton
Chris Waters

Cited quotes were used from the following scholars, historians, and organizations.

James A. Baldwin
Frederick Douglas
William E. Gladstone
Billy Graham
Audrey Hepburn
Lady Bird Johnson
Lyndon B. Johnson
A.P.J. Abdul Kalam
Helen Keller
Dr. Martin Luther King, Jr.
Jess Lair
Nelson Mandela
Margaret Mead
Plato
Jonathan Sacks
Haile Selassie
Charles R. Swindoll
Stacia Tauscher
U.S. National Guard
Andrew Weil

Water Distribution Information
State of Michigan
www.michigan.gov

WATER DISTRIBUTION SITES

http://www.michigan.gov/flintwater/0,6092,7-345-76292_76294_76296---,00.html

Ward 1: Ross Plaza
2320 Pierson St.
Flint, MI 48504

Ward 2: St. Mark Missionary Baptist Church
(closing 8/11/17)
3020 DuPont Street
Flint, MI 48504

Ward 3: Mt. Calvary Missionary Baptist Church
(closing 8/11/17)
4805 N. Saginaw Street
Flint, MI 48505

Ward 4: Franklin Avenue Lot
2804 N. Franklin Avenue
Flint, MI 48506

Ward 5: Old Flint Farmers' Market
(closing 9/5/17)
420 E. Boulevard Drive
Flint, MI 48503

Ward 6: West Court Street Church of God
2920 W. Court Street
Flint, MI 48503

Ward 7: Grace Emmanuel Baptist Church
(closing 9/5/17)
3502 Lapeer Road
Flint, MI 48503

Ward 8: Lincoln Park United Methodist Church
(closing 9/5/17)
3410 Fenton Road
Flint, MI 48507

Ward 9: Eastown Bowl Bowling Alley
3001 S. Dort Highway
Flint, MI 48507

www.ingramcontent.com/pod-product-compliance
Lightning Source LLC
LaVergne TN
LVHW052256100826
845147LV00001B/64

* 9 7 8 0 9 9 8 6 2 2 2 4 8 *